KU-495-766

ENTREPRENEURSHIP AND SMEs IN THE EURO-ZONE

Towards a Theory of Symbiotic Entrepreneurship

ENTREPRENEURSHIP AND SMEs IN THE EURO-ZONE

Towards a Theory of Symbiotic Entrepreneurship

LÉO-PAUL DANA

University of Canterbury, New Zealand

Imperial College Press

Published by

Imperial College Press
57 Shelton Street
Covent Garden
London WC2H 9HE

Distributed by

World Scientific Publishing Co. Pte. Ltd.
5 Toh Tuck Link, Singapore 596224
USA office: 27 Warren Street, Suite 401-402, Hackensack, NJ 07601
UK office: 57 Shelton Street, Covent Garden, London WC2H 9HE

British Library Cataloguing-in-Publication Data
A catalogue record for this book is available from the British Library.

ENTREPRENEURSHIP AND SMEs IN THE EURO-ZONE:
TOWARDS A THEORY OF SYMBIOTIC ENTREPRENEURSHIP

Copyright © 2006 by Imperial College Press

All rights reserved. This book, or parts thereof, may not be reproduced in any form or by any means, electronic or mechanical, including photocopying, recording or any information storage and retrieval system now known or to be invented, without written permission from the Publisher.

For photocopying of material in this volume, please pay a copying fee through the Copyright Clearance Center, Inc., 222 Rosewood Drive, Danvers, MA 01923, USA. In this case permission to photocopy is not required from the publisher.

ISBN 1-86094-647-X   24759872

Typeset by Stallion Press
Email: enquiries@stallionpress.com

Printed in Singapore by World Scientific Printers (S) Pte Ltd

This book is dedicated to Naomi Josephine

About the Author

Léo-Paul Dana is Senior Advisor to the World Association for Small and Medium Enterprises, and tenured at the University of Canterbury. He has also served on the faculties of McGill University and Nanyang Technological University. He was formerly Visiting Professor of Entrepreneurship at INSEAD, and has been Visiting Professor at several business schools across Europe, including the ICN Graduate School of Business, in Nancy, and the Institut d'Administration des Entreprises, at Université Robert Schuman, in Strasbourg. He holds B.A. and M.B.A. degrees from McGill University, and a Ph.D. from the Ecole des Hautes Etudes Commerciales. He has an extensive research background studying entrepreneurship in different cultures and is the author of a number of books and articles on the subject. He is the Founder of the *Journal of International Entrepreneurship*.

Contents

Acknowledgements

The author expresses kind thanks to each member of the Board of Advisors, who assisted with the research involved in the completion of this book.

Board of Advisors

- Pekka AIKIO, President, Sámi Parliament, Finland
- Ulla AIKIO-PUOSKARI, Giellagas Institute, Oulu University, Oulu, Finland
- Simo ALARUIKKA, Enontekiön Kunta, Enontekiö, Finland
- Pia ARENIUS, Université de Lausanne, Lausanne, Switzerland
- Walter BORNETT, Executive Director, Austrian Institute for SME Research, Vienna, Austria
- Guido CAPALDO, Università degli Studi di Napoli Frederico II, Naples, Italy
- Tatiana CHAMEEVA, Bordeaux Business School, France
- Alicia CODURAS, Instituto de Empresa, Madrid, Spain
- Kathleen Osgood DANA, Sterling College, Craftsbury Common, Vermont, USA
- Petra de GROOT, Vrije Universiteit Amsterdam (Free University Amsterdam), The Netherlands
- Pavlos DIMITRATOS, Athens University of Economics and Business, Greece
- Alain FAYOLLE, EM Lyon, France

- Nikolinka FERTALA, University of Tuebingen, Germany
- William B. GARTNER, Clemson University, Clemson, South Carolina, USA
- Dietmar GRICHNIK, Heinrich Heine University, Düsseldorf, Germany
- John GRIN, University of Amsterdam, The Netherlands
- Antonia Madrid GUIJARRO, Universidad Politécnica de Cartegena, Spain
- Graham HALL, Manchester Business School, United Kingdom
- Rachida JUSTO, Vice Dean of Research, Instituto de Empresa, Madrid, Spain
- Hannu KANGASNIEMI, Sámi Parliament, Inari, Finland
- Hugo KANTIS, Universidad Nacional de General Sarmiento, Argentina
- Christian KARITNIG, Fachhochschule Vorarlberg University of Applied Sciences, Dornbirn, Austria
- Alexander KESSLER, Senior Researcher, Austrian Institute for SME Research, Vienna, Austria
- Pertti KETTUNEN, Professor Emeritus, University of Jyväskylä, Finland
- Thomas LACROIX, Université Poitiers, France
- Michel MARCHESNAY, Université de Montpellier 1, France
- Enno MASUREL, Vrije Universiteit Amsterdam (Free University Amsterdam), The Netherlands
- Alberto MATTIACCI, Facoltà di Economia, Università di Siena, Italy
- Asko MIETTINEN, Tampere University of Technology, Tampere, Finland
- Maria MINNITI, Babson College, Wellesley, Massachusetts, USA
- Josef MUGLER, Institut für Betriebswirtschaftslehre der Klein- und Mittelbetriebe, Wirtschaftsuniversität Wien, Vienna, Austria

- Ludger MÜLLER-WILLE, Department of Geography, McGill University, Montreal, Canada
- Emer Ní BHRADAIGH, Dublin City University, Dublin, Ireland
- Jean Jacques OBRECHT, Professor Emeritus, Université Robert Schuman, Strasbourg, France
- Francesco PASTORE, Seconda Università di Napoli, Naples, Italy
- Sandra PENNEWISS, Germany
- Elisabeth PEREIRA, Department of Economics, Management & Industrial Engineering, Universidade de Aveiro, Portugal
- Orlando PETIZ, Minho University, Braga, Portugal
- J. Hanns PICHLER, President, Austrian Institute for SME Research, Vienna, Austria
- Cristina PONSIGLIONE, Università degli Studi di Napoli Frederico II, Naples, Italy
- Ruth RAMA, Spanish Council for Scientific Research, Madrid, Spain
- Jan RATH, University of Amsterdam, The Netherlands
- Liisa REMES, University of Jyväskylä, Jyväskylä, Finland
- Paul Davidson REYNOLDS, London Business School, United Kingdom
- Dietmar ROESSL, Vice President, European Council for Small Business, Vienna University of Economics and Business Administration, Vienna, Austria
- Jan-Florian SCHLAPFNER, Department of Economic and Social Geography, University of Cologne, Cologne, Germany
- Karl-Heinz SCHMIDT, Universität Gesamthochschule, Paderborn, Germany
- Janne SEURUJÄRVI, Director, Inari Municipal Business Company, Ivalo, Finland
- Ana Paula SILVA, Manchester Business School, United Kingdom
- Rolf STERNBERG, Department of Economic and Social Geography, University of Cologne, Cologne, Germany

- Jan ULIJN, Jean Monnet Chair, Eindhoven, The Netherlands
- Sabine URBAN, Université de Strasbourg, France
- Marijke van der VEEN, Dutch Institute for Knowledge Intensive Entrepreneurship, Enschede, The Netherlands
- Daan van SOEST, University of Tilburg, The Netherlands
- Andreas WEH, Fachhochschule Vorarlberg University of Applied Sciences, Dornbirn, Austria
- Isabell WELPE, Ludwig-Maximilians University, Munich, Germany
- Friederike WELTER, Chair, University of Siegen, Germany

Foreword

Writing a book on entrepreneurship in Europe is not an easy task. Focusing on one zone, which seems to be growing toward increased economic and social cohesion and perhaps coherence, where the common currency of the euro has been introduced in January 1, 2002 seems even more of a challenge. The euro-zone comprises 12 countries with a European heritage, but with a large cultural and linguistic diversity including Basque, Finnish, Gaelic, Greek and Sámi tongues. One interesting research hypothesis or question emerges immediately, although it might be not falsifiable or just impossible to test or answer: Has the euro currency contributed to a more universal concept of entrepreneurship leading to the target set for 2010, i.e., making the European Union the most competitive knowledge economy in the world? What if the euro had not been introduced? Is the above diversity the Achilles heel or just the unique Europe opportunity to reach that goal?

An author requires courage to cover such a large set of different views, perceptions and realities about entrepreneurship, even within the limited area of the euro-zone. This might be the reason that the attempts to bring the European business reality into one holistic perspective including the perception by non-European countries and people, when it comes to transgressing the pure economic facts are scarce and cannot be complete (Crane, 2000; Randlesome, 1990). *Mission impossible?* Léo-Paul Dana was probably the best man to take up the gauntlet, since he can be proud of a large track record in researching and writing about entrepreneurship, across the Pacific (1999), the Mediterranean (2000) and from the Balkans to the Baltic states (2005).

The style of this book seems accessible to a broad audience; the manifold quotes do not break up the flow of thought. This volume might also serve as a guide to entrepreneurship. If one has the sharp observation of Léo-Paul Dana, the visuals help to build up this mental picture, backed up by impressive documentation by authors who partly belong to the personal network of the author (see the list of experts, in the Board of Advisors, consulted) for the 12 countries of the present euro-zone.

The concept of entrepreneurship used is somewhat broad: Entrepreneurship is at every street corner or field, literally from the Sámi-country of the reindeer "business" (in Lapland) to Greek entrepreneurship in Germany and Basques entrepreneurs in France, as well as indigenous entrepreneurship in the Irish speaking Gaeltachtaí. This is all part of the euro-zone!

The structure of each chapter helps to make this ambitious comparison of 12 countries transparent: a short introduction with geographic, demographic, and historical overviews, a focus on the economy, entrepreneurship and small business sector and a view on the future. The book is concluded by proposing a label to characterise this European entrepreneurship as a *symbiosis*: Living together with tolerance and respect, but symbiosis is more than "Live and let live." Co-operation is a recurrent item in this book, for instance the notion of collective entrepreneurship in France; not starting a business as an individual venture, but as a team of people rightaway with attention to family business, clustering and networking, such as in Italy and Ireland.

This book brings me to two elements which might be helpful to develop this symbiotic and cooperative entrepreneurship in the future, and probably not only in the euro-zone:

1. It covers a vast literature from hard-to-find sources, but not all entrepreneurship (and innovation) has been published in English and not everything worthwhile has been translated into that

language. Volumes, such as the one in French by Estay and Merdji (2001) about creating and developing a craftsman's company matches nicely what Léo-Paul Dana observes for handicraft entrepreneurship in Greece and Italy. The one in German by Klandt and Brüning (2002) describes the international start-up climate comparing the conditions in nine countries: France, Germany, the Netherlands, Poland, Sweden, the United Kingdom, Malaysia, Singapore and the United States of America. Another (in Dutch) by de Weerd-Nederhof *et al.* (2004) gives a multilevel perspective on the organisation of innovation. This is just to mention three languages in which much entrepreneurship and innovation appear, and any colleague with another native language can easily add pieces of his/her own mother tongue. How can we disclose all this to balance the views and the right mutual perception about entrepreneurship, which rightly can be seen as the engine for new business development and personal welfare and wealth of not only euro-zone citizens? From this perspective, multi-authored publications about European entrepreneurship should be welcomed (see for example, Dana *et al.*, forthcoming).

2. The above reference to innovation brings me to a second element of special care and concern, when it comes to the above-mentioned Lisbon objective in 2010. Léo-Paul Dana could mention for a lot of countries information on the link of entrepreneurship with technical innovation, such as in Finland, France, Ireland, Italy and Spain, but only in passing. The euro-zone is lacking balance across its 12 counties, for not all opportunities and resources are yet used. The over-attention for entrepreneurship and new business development in the ICT sector, whereas other sectors with a strong R&D achievement in the euro-zone are left out (not to be blamed to this courageous book), leads to my hope for more technology entrepreneurship sector-wise, such as a recent example of biotechnology in another part of the world (Hine and Kapeleris, 2005) and a work in preparation by Ulijn and Santema (2006) for the domain of aerospace.

Let us work on symbiotic entrepreneurship in Europe in this sense. Léo-Paul Dana's book can serve both as a companion and a source for inspiration for both research and business practice in the euro-zone, once again due to the unique cultural and linguistic diversity of this subcontinent.

References

Crane, R. (2000), *European Business Cultures*, Harlow, UK: Pearson.

Dana, L. P. (1999), *Entrepreneurship in Pacific Asia*, Singapore, London and Hong Kong: World Scientific.

Dana, L. P. (2000), *Economies of the Eastern Mediterranean Region: Economic Miracles in the Making*, Singapore, London and Hong Kong: World Scientific.

Dana, L. P. (2005), *When Economies Change Hands: A Survey of Entrepreneurship in the Emerging Markets of Europe from the Balkans to the Baltic States,* Binghamton: Haworth.

Dana, L. P., M. Han, V. Ratten, and I. Welpe, eds. (forthcoming), *A Theory of Internationalisation for European Entrepreneurship*, Cheltenham: Edward Elgar.

De Weerd-Nederhof, P., B. Van Looy, and K. Visscher (2004), *Innovatie(f) organiseren*, Deventer: Kluwer.

Estay, C., and M. Merdji (2001), *Créer et développer une entreprise artisanale,* Paris: Dunod.

Hine, D., and J. Kapeleris (2005), *Innovation and Entrepreneurship in Biotechnology, an International Perspective: Concepts, Theories and Cases*, Cheltenham: Edward Elgar.

Klandt, H., and E. Brüning (2002), *Das internationale Gründungsklima: Neun Länder im Vergleich ihrer Rahmenbedingungen für Existenz- und Unternehmensgründungen*, Berlin: Duncker & Humblot.

Randlesome, C. (1990), *Business Cultures in Europe*, Oxford: Heinemann.

Ulijn, J., and S. C. Santema (2006), *Aerospace Management and Organisation: The Case of Innovation, Entrepreneurship and Culture*, Delft Series of AOM, Volume 1, Cheltenham: Edward Elgar.

Professor Dr. Jan Ulijn
Jean Monnet Chair in Innovation, Entrepreneurship and Culture
Eindhoven University of Technology
The Netherlands
September 25, 2005

Chapter 1

Introduction

1.1 *Introduction*

"Entrepreneurship was born in Europe (Fayolle *et al.*, 2005, p. 4)." In fact the concept of the entrepreneur first appeared in 1437 in a French dictionary (Landström, 1999). Yet, Groen *et al.* (2006) suggested that entrepreneurship has been so far very much an American concept. Nevertheless, entrepreneurship in Europe is gaining importance, as is the small business sector. According to Mugler (1998), the renaissance of the small business sector in Europe has been a spill-over of the sector's revival initiated in the United States.

The European Charter for Small Enterprises, adopted by the General Affairs Council, recognises that small firms are the backbone of the European economy. Reynolds (1997) noted that the expansion of markets has not been associated with an expanded role for larger firms; instead, smaller firms are filling niche roles (Malaise, 1988; Buckley, 1997). Fotopoulos and Spence (1998) suggested that small firms use survival strategies and overcome barriers to entry, and Kemp and Lutz (2006) found that micro-firms perceive lower barriers to entry than medium-sized and large businesses. In fact, society needs Small and Medium Enterprises (SMEs) to undertake functions that multinationals do not do because of the opportunity cost involved. It is often uneconomical for a large firm to produce a small run. This is where self-employed entrepreneurs can excel in niche markets.

1

The purpose of this book is to provide a brief overview of self-employment in selected countries (the first to use the euro as their currency), along with a brief description of the environments in which entrepreneurs operate. As discussed by Kaynak and Jallat, this "will necessitate consideration of the broader social, cultural and legal-political systems (2004, p. 5)." Brief historical overviews will also be provided, because, "Progress, far from consisting in change, depends on retentiveness. When change is absolute there remains no being to improve and no direction is set for possible improvement... Those who cannot remember the past are condemned to repeat it (Santayana, 1905, Volume 1, p. 284)."

Given the vastness of Europe and its diversity, focus will be only on the original 12 countries that adopted the euro[1] as their currency. It will be shown that the euro-zone is *not* a monolith market — but a union of diverse markets of different sizes and importance, *with different styles of entrepreneurship*. Savitt (1998) suggested understanding the differences before attempting to find similarities. As noted by Ulijn and Fayolle (2004), people from one euro-zone country tend to value self-employment over employment, while the opposite is true in another country of the euro-zone. Along the same lines, Obrecht (2005) argued that the cultural environment affects entrepreneurial capabilities.

Abandoning a national currency in favour of a regional one has many implications. The euro became a sure thing relatively recently. Javetski and Templeman wrote, "The certainty of German unification has already sidetracked Europe's plans to have a single market functioning by 1992, and it has buried an ambitious, French-backed scheme to create a new European currency. If there's a substitute money in Europe's future now, it's probably the Deutschemark (1990, p. 48)." Now that we have the euro, are countries becoming less different from one another? Is entrepreneurship becoming more similar across nations?

---

[1]The plural of euro is the same as the singular.

At the macro-economic level, Europe is experiencing convergence; technology, for instance, is becoming increasingly similar in different countries. At the micro-level, however, Europeans from different regions are maintaining cultural uniqueness. As observed by Berlinski, "Unsurprisingly, it is difficult to cobble nation-states together into a grand transnational entity (2005, p. A-17)." Entrepreneurship is also maintaining regional characteristics, but co-operation, networking and clustering into industrial agglomerations (Baptista and Swann, 1998; Glassman and Voelzkow, 2001) is becoming very important across the euro-zone. This book will suggest that formerly independent entrepreneurs are increasingly collaborating for mutual benefit, creating symbiotic entrepreneurship.

1.2   *Definitions*

Cantillon (1755) defined the French word *entrepreneur* as any person taking the risk to work for oneself. The aristocrat industrialist, Jean Baptiste Say defined the entrepreneur as the agent who "unites all means of production and who finds in the value of the products... the re-establishment of the entire capital he employs, and the value of the wages, the interest, and the rent which he pays, as well as the profits belonging to himself (1816, pp. 28–29)." Fraser (1937) associated entrepreneurs with the management of a business unit, profit taking, business innovation and uncertainty bearing. Belshaw argued, "An entrepreneur is someone who takes the initiative in administering resources." He explained, "He is probably not an entrepreneur unless he does undertake ordinary management tasks (Belshaw, 1955, p. 147)." There are countless definitions of entrepreneurship, and the same is true of SMEs. In Australia, small firms have fewer than 20 employees, except small manufacturers which have up to 99. In Canada, a small service firm has up to 49 employees, while a small manufacturer may have up to 499. In Japan, a firm with up to 250 employees is deemed to be small. In the United States, a small business may have up to 500 employees.

Until 1996, the European Union defined an SME as fewer than 500 employees. In April 1996, the European Commission adopted the following[2] definitions:

- SMEs are independent firms with fewer than 250 employees and have either an annual turnover not exceeding ECU[3] 40 million, or a balance sheet total not exceeding ECU 27 million.
- The small enterprise has fewer than 50 employees and has either an annual turnover not exceeding ECU 7 million or an annual balance-sheet total not exceeding ECU 5 million and conforms to criterion of independence.
- Independent enterprises are those which are not owned as 25% or more of the capital or the voting rights by one enterprise, or jointly by several enterprises, falling outside the definition of an SME or a small enterprise, whichever may apply.

Among several later definitions, SMEs were defined as independent firms (i.e., other companies' share of ownership could not exceed 25%), with fewer than 250 employees, and annual sales not exceeding 20,000,000 euro. Since January 1, 2005, European Commission definitions have been as follows:

- Micro-enterprises are firms with up to nine employees and annual sales of less than 2,000,000 euro.
- Small businesses have between 11 and 50 employees inclusively, and sales of up to 10,000,000 euro.
- Medium-sized enterprises have over 50, and up to 250 employees, with sales not exceeding 50 million euro.

In this book, the word "entrepreneurship" refers to the economic undertaking of entrepreneurs. This is based on the classical definition of

---

[2] Source: European Commission Recommendation 96/280/EC.
[3] The European Currency Unit (ECU) was the predecessor of the euro.

the word, which can be traced to the German *unternehmung* (literally: undertaking) and to the French *entreprendre* (literally: between taking). The agents of entrepreneurship are entrepreneurs (from the French *entrepreneurs,* literally: between takers). The word "entrepreneur" will be used in the context of a self-employed founder or owner of a business entity, usually a small or medium firm and sometimes a large one. Given that Schumpeterian (1934) innovators are relatively few, this book accepts the notion that SMEs comprise the more common flagship of entrepreneurship — as described by Cantillon (1755) — in the broadest sense.

1.3 *Toward the Euro*

Europe, with more countries in fewer square kilometres than anywhere else in the world, has a long history of free trade agreements. When Nuremburg was a city-state in the Roman Empire, it set up free trade agreements with 70 other entities; although it lacked a good waterway, arable land and natural resources, its free trade agreements enabled it to become a cosmopolitan business centre.

Over the years, economic power shifted across Europe. Sombart noted, "One of the most important facts in the growth of modern economic life is the removal of the centre of economic activity from the nations of Southern Europe — the Italians, Spaniards, and Portuguese, with whom must be reckoned some South German lands — to those of the North-West — the Dutch, the French, the English and the North Germans (1913, p. 11)."

In 1834, several German states formed a union for free trade — *Zollverein.* Italy and San Marino formed a customs union in 1862. In 1921, Belgium, the Netherlands and Luxembourg entered the Benelux customs union. In 1951, Belgium, France, the Federal Republic of Germany, Italy, Luxembourg and the Netherlands signed the Treaty of Paris creating the European Coal and Steel Community. The 1957

Treaty of Rome came into effect on January 1, 1958, establishing the European Common Market (later the European Economic Community), uniting Belgium, France, the Federal Republic of Germany, Italy, Luxembourg and the Netherlands.

In 1959, the Stockholm convention established the European Free Trade Association (EFTA), allowing Austria, Iceland, Norway, Sweden and Switzerland to maintain different external tariffs while eliminating internal tariffs on industrial products originating within the free trade area. Finland joined EFTA in 1961.

In 1973, the European Economic Community welcomed the Kingdom of Denmark, the Republic of Ireland and the United Kingdom of Great Britain and Northern Ireland. Greece joined in 1981, followed by Portugal and Spain in 1986. In 1989, the Council of Ministers of the European Economic Community adopted the decision to make SMEs a priority. This included the creation of a favourable environment with limited regulation, the encouragement of new venture creation and the establishment of R&D priorities. In 1991, the Maastricht Treaty laid the foundation for an Economic and Monetary Union (EMU).

In 1993, the Single European Act created a European Union allowing free movement of goods, services, capital and labour. At the time there were 17 million privately-owned enterprises in the non-primary sector of the European Union, of which 93.3% were micro firms, 6.2% were small, 0.5% were medium, and 0.1% were large (Mulhern, 1995). Potts argued that the concept of a single European market was supported by, "to be accurate, big business more than small business (2000, p. 322)." In 1995, the Union grew with the entry of three former members of EFTA, namely Austria, Finland and Sweden.

On January 1, 2002, 12 of the 15 members of the European Union began using the euro. (Three kingdoms — Denmark, Sweden and the United Kingdom — opted not to adopt the euro at that time.) Fifty billion coins were struck and 14.5 billion notes were printed.

1.4   *Diversity in a United Europe*

Does enterprise develop the same way amongst all peoples? Farmer and Richman explained, "The sociological or cultural environment of a country has an impact on the ways in which industrial enterprises and their personnel carry out their functions (1965, p. 109)." They then discussed "the *dominant* human attitudes, values and beliefs in a given society or country and the way they tend to influence the motivation, behaviour and performance of individuals working in productive enterprises (Farmer and Richman, 1965, p. 109)." For example, "In the first half of 1976, the total days lost by strikes per 1,000 workers was... 177 in France, but the German rate was only 19 (Putman, 1977, pp. 158–159)."

Farmer and Richman elaborated, "Prevailing religious beliefs and cultural values, in conjunction with parental behaviour, child-rearing practices, and the formal system of education in a particular country, usually have a direct and very significant bearing on the dominant view toward work and achievement (1965, pp. 156–157)." Farmer and Richman also addressed the issue that, "Since there may be various subcultures in a particular country, research in this area can be very complex (1965, pp. 109–110)." Discussing subculture, Jennings reported about an interviewer who explained to him that, "The Bavarians shoot slower than the Prussians (1974, p. 413)."

Hofstede (1980) examined cultural differences, and based on research with INSEAD Executive Development students, Laurent concluded, "Deep seated managerial assumptions are strongly shaped by national cultures and appear quite insensitive to the more transient culture of organisations (1983, p. 75)." Huntington (1993; 1996) and more recently Marsh (2004) argued that globalisation has neither standardised societies, nor produced a homogeneous world culture. Neither will the euro.

Entrepreneurship exists around the world; yet, it is far from standardised. Entrepreneurship means different things to different people. In recent years, there has been increasing interest in comparing entrepreneurs from different cultures. Scheinberg and MacMillan (1988) found significant differences across cultures in motivations to launch a new business. Dana (1995a) concluded that entrepreneurship was not simply a function of opportunity recognition in isolation, but coloured by cultural perception of opportunity. As noted by Aldrich (1999), the environment constitutes the initial conditions facing the entrepreneur.

Of course, people from different ethnic backgrounds have been exposed to dissimilar cultural values, and this is reflected in their respective entrepreneurship models. Various cultural aspects, such as the social value ascribed to the entrepreneur, attitudes toward the risk of failure and the presence of exemplary entrepreneurial models are cultural factors that have an impact on the formation of the entrepreneurial calling (McGrath *et al.*, 1992; Wennekers and Thurik, 2001).

Also important is the role of the state. Spencer *et al.* (2005) described Finland as having a Social corporatist institutional structure with the state playing a facilitative role; in contrast, they described Germany as a country as having a State corporatist structure, in which "networks among organised social actors may equilibrate state centralism (2005, p. 326)." They grouped Belgium, France and Italy as having political and managerial leaders who "tend to cooperate rather than act as adversaries (Spencer *et al.*, 2005, p. 326)."

Entrepreneurship is therefore *not* homogeneous around the world, or within Europe, or even within the euro-zone. As Pascal (1701) explained, that which is truth on one side of the Pyrenees is not so on the other. His sister quoted his exact words, "Vérité en deçà des Pyrénées, erreur au-delà (Perier, 1842, p. 61)."

1.5   *Different Contexts for Enterprise*

Up to the late 1970s, government policies in Europe tended to encourage mergers of existing firms into larger units (Strinati, 1982). In 1974, for example, the state firm Aeroporti di Roma was formed, absorbing about 60 SMEs. Scase (1980) noted that the trend in Europe was to evolve away from small independent businesses, as governments believed instead that a measure to facilitate economic growth would be to encourage a close partnership between the existing large firms in the private sector and state agencies. More recently, the trend has been for the state to recognise the usefulness of entrepreneurs, and an environment fostering entrepreneurship.

As demonstrated by Rainnie and Scott (1986), entrepreneurship became increasingly recognised as a means of improving output and as discussed by Scase and Goffee (1987), the policy of some governments gradually shifted from discouraging to encouraging independent business. Entrepreneurship has been recognised as being in the national interest, making important contributions to economic expansion and job creation.

Nevertheless, while governments have raced to promote entrepreneurship and innovation, there has been a lack of consensus about the means to attain this objective (Dana, 1987). Among the environmental factors that powerfully condition the ease and scope of entrepreneurial activity, are government, laws, regulations and procedures (Staley and Morse, 1971). Furthermore, government policy reflects the attitude of legislators. One can identify two broad models to which government policies belong:

Model I, Regulation for Protection:
Rules are established to protect existing business — even if this hinders entrepreneurial behaviour. This is the model adopted by many countries such as France, where regulation has been instituted to protect firms, as well as consumers.

Model II, Protection from Regulation:
A policy of minimal intervention and minimal regulation allows entrepreneurs to dedicate more resources to their enterprises, protecting

them from the burden of excessive paperwork requirements and the constraints of heavy regulations.

The nature of intervention by a government (through regulations, paperwork requirements, subsidies, trade agreements, etc.) affects entrepreneurship and innovation. Peterson and Peterson (1981) showed that government paperwork requirements can be a burden on managerial time of owner-managers. In contrast, the state may foster entrepreneurship by creating an inviting environment for enterprise. The following 12 chapters shall provide brief overviews of entrepreneurship across the euro-zone.

Chapter 2

Austria

2.1 *Introduction*

Austria is a federal republic, covering 83,858 square kilometres, border-ing the Czech Republic,[1] Germany,[2] Hungary,[3] Italy,[4] Liechtenstein,[5] Slovakia,[6] Slovenia[7] and Switzerland.[8] Small business has a long history in Austria. According to McMillan, "Mozart earned his living as an entrepreneur in the marketplace (2002, p. 26)." Bolton and Thompson described Mozart as "both a genius and an entrepreneur (2004, p. 229)." Mozart was born in Salzburg (see Exhibit 2.1).

Austrian economists — especially Schumpeter (1934) — can be seen as precursors of entrepreneurship research. Yet, Haberfellner (2003) argued that Austria was still a highly regulated economy and described Austria as a corporatist country in which entrepreneurship was some-what limited. Comparing Austria with France, Ulijn and Fayolle wrote that in contrast to French people who tend to value self-employment over employment, Austrians "prefer the employment and not the self-employment status (2004, p. 211)." Miles *et al.* (2005) observed that

---

[1] For a discussion of entrepreneurs and small business in the Czech Republic, see Dana (2000c; 2005b).
[2] See Chapter 6 in this book.
[3] See Dana (2005b).
[4] See Chapter 9 in this book.
[5] See Dana and Dana (2003).
[6] See Dana (2000c; 2005b).
[7] See Dana (2005b).
[8] See Dana *et al.* (forthcoming).

Exhibit 2.1   Salzburg; photo © 2005 Léo-Paul Dana

although there are still some complex and slow bureaucratic procedures, the role of the state in the economy has been decreasing. The influence of the Church is also less prominent than was the case in former times (see Exhibit 2.2).

2.2   *Historical Overview*

In 1273, the Count of Habsburg conquered Austria — *Österreich* (literally Eastern Kingdom) — which his descendants would rule for many generations. During the 16th century, the Habsburg dynasty acquired Bohemia, Spain and parts of Hungary and Italy as well.

Ehmer (1997) provided an account of 18th century artisans in Vienna. In 1804, the Habsburgs adopted the title of emperor; Vienna served as the imperial capital. In 1867, a dual monarchy was created, including Hungary in addition to Austria (see Exhibit 2.3). The year 1874 saw the construction of the famous Hofburgtheater (see

Exhibit 2.2   Church in Dornbirn; photo © 2005 Léo-Paul Dana

Exhibit 2.4) in Vienna. In 1878, the Ottoman provinces of Bosnia and Herzegovina were added to the Empire as a protectorate, and annexed in 1908 (see Dana, 1999b).

On November 12, 1918, following the collapse of the Austro-Hungarian Empire, Austria was proclaimed a republic, within today's borders. Bachinger (1987) described the economic situation of the

Exhibit 2.3   Belvedere Palace; photo © 2005 Léo-Paul Dana

Exhibit 2.4   The Hofburgtheater; photo © 2005 Léo-Paul Dana

Austrian relict of the Habsburg monarchy. An energy crisis was coupled with a food shortage, while the debasement of the currency accompanied an unstable political situation. However, the weak currency favoured exports, and Austria experienced remarkable economic growth until the Great Depression. Chater (1929) provided an account of inter-war Austria.

The republic was short-lived as Austria was annexed into the German Reich in 1938. During World War II the Nazis took over all industry of significant size in Austria. Following the war, a provisional government was set up on April 27, 1945. As noted by Dana (1992a), one in three Austrians worked on a farm in 1945.

In 1948, the European Recovery Programme began pumping investments and new life in Austria. In his discussion of prices and salaries, Long noted "the average in Vienna last summer being 730 schillings ($28) a month (1951, p. 752)."

Until 1955, Austria was administered as four zones, occupied by France, the United Kingdom of Great Britain and Northern Ireland, the United States of America and the Union of Soviet Socialist Republics. Austria recovered full independence in 1955. Austrian economic policy envisaged a reconstruction based on large firms and reconstruction took place at an amazing pace (see Exhibit 2.5); a discussion appears in Bowie (1959). In 1964, Innsbruck (see Exhibit 2.6) hosted the Winter Olympics.

The self-employment rate for Austrians, especially in agriculture, fell sharply between the 1980s and the 1990s (Haberfellner, 2003). Entrepreneurship research studies analysing the early 1990s indicated that Austria had low self-employment and start-up rates (Austrian Institute for SME Research, 1996). Yet, start-ups were found to have high survival rates (Wanzenböck, 1998). With this in mind, the Austrian government established numerous initiatives to increase the relevance of entrepreneurship. This included campaigns promoting self-employment in the media, the establishment of university chairs and

Exhibit 2.5   Damaged by WWII, the Urania was Rebuilt by 1957; photo © 2005 Léo-Paul Dana

Exhibit 2.6   Innsbruck, in the Centre of the Tyrol Province; photo © 2005 Léo-Paul Dana

programmes of emphasis for entrepreneurship at schools, business plan competitions, a reduction of bureaucratic procedures and support programmes for start-ups. During the late 1990s start-up rates and rates of self-employment began rising significantly. While the number of start-ups was between 14,000 and 15,000 during the period from 1993 to 1995, the number for 2004 rose to nearly 30,000 (Wirtschaftskammern Österreichs, 2005, p. 8).

In 2002, approximately 28,000 new enterprises were founded in Austria. One third out of these reflected the net growth in the number of companies, while the other two thirds were substitutes for other, closing companies (Getzner *et al.*, 2004, p. 16).

The rate of self-employment (excluding agriculture) rose from 7.2% in 1990 to 8% in 2003. According to the Austrian Federal Economic Chamber, self-employment outside the agricultural sector was 7.9% of the workforce in 2003 (Wirtschaftskammern Österreichs, 2003, p. 25). That year, Austria's per capita GDP was 26,900 euro, placing it in fourth place among the 25 member-states of the European Union (after Luxembourg, Ireland and Denmark). The unemployment rate in Austria during 2003 was 4.5%, the second lowest after Cyprus within the EU25; this was relatively low when compared to the average of the EU25 with 9%, or the United States with 6% (Wirtschaftskammern Österreichs, 2004, p. 17). Yet, economic growth in 2004 was only 1.8%, while the total growth of the EU25 was 2.1% (Wirtschaftskammern Österreichs, 2004, p. 13). This may be a result of the weak economy of Germany[9] — the most important export market for Austria. While the number of textile factories (see Exhibit 2.7) and food-processing firms has been decreasing in Austria, *Gewerbe* (craft) and service enterprises have been on the rise. About four fifths of the craft businesses are family-owned.

---

[9]See Landler (2005).

Exhibit 2.7   A Former Textile Factory; photo © 2005 Léo-Paul Dana

According to first longitudinal studies analysing the development of start-ups during the years 1996 and later (Frank *et al.*, 2002, p. 33; Schwarz and Grieshuber, 2003, p. 19), survival rates did not suffer from the higher number of start-ups; the higher quantity of start-ups did not cause a lower quality of the start-ups when measured by survival rates.

2.3   *The Economy, Entrepreneurship & the Small Business Sector*

The Austrian Industrial Code defines business as any independent, continuous activity carried out for profit, excluding learned and artistic professions and other exceptions. Most Austrian SMEs are family businesses (see Exhibit 2.8). Due to the physical terrain of the Alps, much land is difficult to cultivate, and farms in Austria tend to be much smaller than those in Germany and tiny when compared to American farms.

SMEs constitute the backbone of the economy, in large and small towns alike (see Exhibit 2.9). More than 210,000 enterprises employ over 1.5 million people. According to the medium-sized businesses

Exhibit 2.8   Family Businesses Abound; photo © 2005 Léo-Paul Dana

report 2002/03 of the Federal Ministry of Economy and Labour, 99.5% of the enterprises in Austria are SMEs, as per the European Union definition, including firms with up to 249 employees. These firms employ 65% of the Austrian labour force and produce 58% of total income. Furthermore, they provide about 80% of Austria's income tax revenues, and about 70% of the total revenue of sales tax. Austrian SMEs are especially remarkable, considering that a long lasting economic malaise did not result in job losses in the SME sector; instead, the number of jobs provided by SMEs increased by about 8% between 1995 and 2003 (Pichler and Bornett, 2005). Compared with other countries in Europe, Austria has a particularly high rate of small (10–49 employees) and medium-sized (50–249 employees) enterprises, while the share of micro-enterprises (up to 9 employees) and large enterprises (more than 249 employees) is comparatively low (Pichler and Bornett, 2005, p. 123).

Exhibit 2.9   Graz; photo © 2005 Léo-Paul Dana

With regards to the number of enterprises, commerce was the leading sector in 2003 with 29% of all enterprises, followed by economic services and tourism (each with 18%) and manufacturing (12%); due to a superior average size of enterprises, the latter sector provides the highest share of jobs (24%), followed by commerce (24%) and economic services (14%).[10]

Fewer than 1,000 major enterprises employ 815,000 people. Within the SME sector about 473,000 people work in companies with 50 to 249 employees. Approximately 530,000 persons are employed in enterprises with 10 to 49 employees and about 500,000 persons in the so called smallest-enterprises with less than 10 employees. Between 1995 and 2003 the number of SMEs rose by 11.6%. The highest increase was noted by the smallest-companies. The growth in the production

---

[10]Source: Pichler and Bornett, 2005, p. 126.

and service sector was mainly the result of SMEs (Bundesministerium für Wirtschaft und Arbeit, 2005, p. 69f).

In general, Austria offers a SME-friendly environment. Several public institutions support the establishment and expansion of new ventures. These include the Austria Wirtschaftsservice GmbH, the economic departments of every provincial government and the Austrian Federal Economic Chamber[11] with its subsidiaries in each federal region. (There are important regional differences, and variations between urban and rural regions — see Exhibit 2.10). Well-networked, such institutions offer support with business planning and assistance with risk evaluation. Moreover, they conduct market research and provide the results in exchange for a nominal fee. In addition, the state provides grants and loans to entrepreneurs. Also worth mentioning are various organisations, such as the *Industriellenvereinigung* (industrial association), that lobby to enforce the interests of the entrepreneurs at a political level.

Arguing that Austria was highly regulated, Haberfellner (2003) noted the decision by the Federal Economic Chamber to implement a quota on the number of Eastern European entrepreneurs operating in Austria. A considerable number of immigrants from Turkey and from the former Yugoslav republics have become self-employed in Austria, largely in the retail and catering sectors — both of which have low barriers to entry.

Sub-contracting is important for SMEs in Austria. Austria's Ministry of Economy and Labour has helped establish the Association of Austrian Sub-contractors, which in turn facilitates matchmaking; the result is a *symbiotic interdependence* among partners in international alliances.

Several institutions, along with the Austrian Ministry of Economy and Labour, have been quite creative with regards to the

---

[11] Membership in this Chamber is compulsory for all Austrian companies.

Exhibit 2.10   Vorarlberg is One of Nine Provinces; photo © 2005 Léo-Paul Dana

internationalisation of Austrian SMEs. This includes project guarantees, financing guarantees and export risk guarantees available to small-scale exporters.

The Federal Economic Chamber has an *Exportakademie*, which offers courses in internationalisation and foreign languages. The Chamber also has Economic Promotion Institutes that provide training and consultancy to entrepreneurs, as well as subsidies for advertising and participating in trade fairs abroad. In addition, the Chamber has established a fund to help cover eventual losses of entrepreneurs who opt to internationalise their operations, with the objective of strengthening competitiveness in foreign markets.

The *Österreichische Kontrollbank* administers export guarantee schemes against economic and political risks. SMEs are entitled to loans at special conditions; these are administered by the Austrian Export-Fonds GmbH. There is also a special export financing scheme (*Export-finanzierungsverfahren*). Export intensity in 2002 was 35.6% of GDP, ranking Austria among the upper third in an international comparison (Wirtschaftskammern Österreichs, 2003, p. 7).

2.4   *Toward the Future*

Ninety-eight percent of firms in Austria have fewer than 50 employees and approximately 56% of employees in this country work in such small firms.[12] Liberalisation of trade has encouraged an increase in specialisation, and low-technology labour-intensive production is being transferred abroad (often to Eastern Europe[13]), in favour of value-adding opportunities. As a result, the services sector has been growing considerably, while the number of Austrian SMEs in textiles has been decreasing. Yet, Turkish entrepreneurs *often with networks in Turkey* are heavily involved in Austria's garment sector. Such trends are likely to continue, reflecting differences in labour costs.

Situated in the heart of Europe, Austria's geographical situation, its closeness to Eastern Europe and the possibilities of *cost-efficient outsourcing opportunities can be very advantageous for Austrian entrepreneurs.* High technical standards in Austria, an excellent infrastructure and the quality of the education (see Exhibit 2.11) system are additional assets. Less attractive are the tax-system, the bureaucracy and (compared to other European countries) high labour costs (Wirtschaftskammern Österreichs, 2003, p. 27f). While Austria is a suitable business location

---

[12] Source: EU European Observatory of SMEs.
[13] See Dana (2005b).

Exhibit 2.11   Fachhochschule Vorarlberg Offers Entrepreneurship Training; photo © 2005 Léo-Paul Dana

for service and engineering enterprises, high labour and living costs (see Exhibit 2.12) make Austria less attractive for labour-intensive firms requiring unskilled labour.

Entrepreneurs in Austria appear to be increasingly focused or specialised. A trend has been the reduction of start-up sizes, measured by employees. There has been significant growth in the number of one-person-firms. A study of the Tyrol province — one of the nine in Austria — showed that in 2004, 41.4% of the members of the regional economic chamber (membership in the economic chamber is compulsory for all Austrian companies) were one-person-firms without any employees (Beyer *et al.*, 2005).

The government intends to become more customer-orientated when dealing with entrepreneurs. Plans are to reduce bureaucracy and thus to avoid entry barriers while attracting new enterprisers. Tax reductions have been taking effect (corporation tax was reduced from 34%

Exhibit 2.12   Pensioner Supplements His Income; photo © 2005 Léo-Paul Dana

to 25%), and investments are being funnelled into research centres, business parks and business incubators. Meanwhile, the educational system is adapting to the changing requirements of the economy.

For the decade from 2004 to 2013, Mandl (2004) predicted that some 51,500 Austrian SMEs with approximately 440,000 employees will be up for succession or transfer. This represents nearly one quarter of all Austrian businesses. Most business successions are carried out within a family; the prime motive is generational change. However, analyses suggested — due to negative equity capital — about 9% of these enterprises are not qualified for transfer.

Chapter 3

Belgium

3.1 *Introduction*

Belgium covers 30,528 square kilometres, bordering France, Germany, Luxembourg and the Netherlands. The kingdom is a multicultural federal state, consisting of three linguistic communities (Dutch, French and German) and three regions: (i) bilingual Brussels (see Exhibit 3.1); (ii) Flanders, which is the Flemish region, and (iii) Wallonia, the Walloon region, which includes French and German speakers. While the Flemish people are Germanic, the Walloons trace their origins to Romanised Celts. Brussels is an important business centre (see Exhibit 3.2) and the national capital, as well as capital of the European Union. The oldest citizen of Brussels, the Manneken-Pis (see Exhibit 3.3) is considered to be the popular protector of Brussels.

Belgium was the first country on the continent to experience the industrial revolution (Kossman-Putto and Kossman, 1996). Today, the nation is a world leader in research and development transfer, with close co-operation between researchers and industry. In Flanders, a government campaign has encouraged entrepreneurs to translate research into new products. In Wallonia, the state has implemented its *quatre par quatre pour entreprendre* initiative. This includes creating awareness of entrepreneurship, fostering new venture creation, providing assistance to enterprises and improving corporate governance. Yet, *The Global Entrepreneurship Monitor Executive Report for Belgium & Wallonia* suggested, "It can be seen that the social and cultural norms in Belgium

Exhibit 3.1   Place de Brouckere; photo © 2005 Léo-Paul Dana

Exhibit 3.2   Stock Exchange; photo © 2005 Léo-Paul Dana

Exhibit 3.3   Manneken-Pis; photo © 2005 Léo-Paul Dana

are not very supportive for entrepreneurship (De Clercq *et al.*, 2004, p. 70)."

3.2   *Historical Overview*

In 1519, the area which is now Belgium came under Spanish rule, and in 1555 Philip II ascended to the throne, ushering in an era of Spanish Inquisitions. For Antwerp, the economic heart of Flanders, prosperity came to an end in 1585 when Antwerp surrendered to the Spanish army, and wealthy citizens moved north to the Netherlands. Sombart wrote, "Antwerp lost no small part of its former glory by reason of the departure of the Jews, and in the 17th century especially it was realised how much they contributed to bring about material prosperity (1913, p. 19)." Today, Brussels has an important Jewish community (see Exhibit 3.4), as does Antwerp.

Exhibit 3.4   Synagogue in Brussels; photo © 2005 Léo-Paul Dana

The Southern Netherlands remained under Spanish rule until 1700. In 1713, the region fell under Austrian rule and Antwerp[1] (see Exhibit 3.5) prospered once again as the economic and commercial centre of Flanders. In 1794, this land was annexed to France and the Belgian textile industry prospered, possibly because Napoleon had banned the imports of English cloth. The merger with France did not last long, however. In 1815, the Congress of Vienna incorporated Belgian lands

---

[1] For a discussion of Antwerp as an international diamond centre, see Chater (1925).

Exhibit 3.5   Antwerp; photo © 2005 Léo-Paul Dana

into the Kingdom of the United Netherlands, with William of Orange on the throne.

Belgium became a country after it decreed its independence from the Netherlands in 1830. The following year, Prince Leopold of Saxe-Coburg was elected king by a national congress. In 1839, the Treaty of London established peace with the Netherlands. Leopold II succeeded his father in 1865.

Formerly a personal possession of the king, the Belgian Congo was taken over by the kingdom in 1907. The Congo Free State became a colony in 1908.

When King Leopold died in 1909, he was succeeded by his nephew, Albert I, who became a hero of the Great War (World War I) after the German invasion of August 1914. Chater (1925) gave an account of Belgium after the war.

Between the World Wars, Brussels was considered "a typical buffer state between the Great Powers represented by France on the one hand and Germany on the other (Stamp, 1939, p. 360)." Chandler (1938) described Belgium shortly before World War II. The Nazis invaded in 1940 and Leopold III was interned.

Klemmer (1948) noted that Belgium served as a battleground for some of the fiercest fighting of World War II, and that during Nazi occupation Belgians lived on fewer than 1,300 calories a day. He was impressed with the fast recovery of the economy: "Meat was derationed on February 1, 1948, leaving only coal, sugar, fats, and cereals still subject to control. Belgian industry, always dynamic, is operating at more than 100% of the pre-war level (1948, p. 575)."

In 1951, King Leopold III abdicated in favour of his son Baudouin. Marden (1955) focused on post-war Bruges (see Exhibit 3.6), describing this town as the heart of Flanders. In 1958, Brussels hosted the 1958 World Fair, a feature of which was the Atomium (see Exhibit 3.7).[2]

Pang noted, "There was a decrease in self-employment in the post-war period from 1947 to 1980. This might be explained by the new welfare state with its safety net and economic expansion, which guaranteed nearly full employment until the early 1970s. With the recession it is argued that households, mainstream and immigrant alike, were driven into self-employment as a survival strategy (2003, p. 208)."

---

[2] For a discussion, see Walker (1958).

Exhibit 3.9   Sud-Est SE-210 Caravelle; photo courtesy of SABENA

3.3   *The Economy, Entrepreneurship & the Small Business Sector*

De Clercq *et al.* wrote, "Until some years ago, entrepreneurs had a very bad image and the image as a whole was very bad (2004, p. 72)."

In 2001, Belgium ranked as the least entrepreneurial country out of the 29 participants in the Global Entrepreneurship Monitor (GEM) research project. Entrepreneurial activity declined by 35% from 2001 to 2002. Simultaneously, the proportion of female entrepreneurs to male entrepreneurs dropped dramatically. In the 2002 report, De Clercq *et al.* observed, "In 2002, across all GEM countries, men were about 50% more likely to be involved in entrepreneurial activity than women. In Belgium, men were about three times more likely to be involved than women (2002, p. 25.)" They elaborated, "Further, there was a strong notion that starting a business is not a socially accepted option for Belgian women (De Clercq *et al.*, 2002, p. 26)."

The study also found that "Belgian entrepreneurs were older than in the rest of the world. Almost 40% of the Belgian entrepreneurs were between 35 and 44 years old, while the age group between 25 and 34 was the most important one worldwide (De Clercq *et al.*, 2002, p. 24)." Another interesting finding was that, "Entrepreneurs lack communication skills (De Clercq *et al.*, 2002, p. 39)."

The following GEM study showed an increase in entrepreneurial activity over the preceding year. De Clercq *et al.* noted, "Belgium seems to be somewhat more entrepreneurial than France, Finland, Italy and the Netherlands... The Walloon figure is somewhat higher than the Belgian average (2004, p. 3)." Findings showed that 75% of all Belgian entrepreneurs, and almost 85% of all Walloon entrepreneurs were men. The authors suggested, "The picture is even more worrying when analysing the type of companies that men and women start. As many men as women start a company out of necessity in Wallonia... In Belgium as a whole, there are even slightly more women entrepreneurs who start a company out of necessity than men. This further implies that the discrepancy between male and female entrepreneurs is even higher for opportunity entrepreneurship (De Clercq *et al.*, 2004, p. 48)."

About one fifth of all Walloon opportunity entrepreneurs are older than 55. The authors suggested, "This shows that entrepreneurship can be seen as a viable alternative to end one's career. For Belgium as a whole, this can be seen as an interesting route to activate adults who had retired early, but who have invaluable experience and expertise (De Clercq *et al.*, 2004, p. 50)."

With regards to job creation, the study revealed, "Only 5% of the Belgian starters created more than 20 jobs. The results for Wallonia show that none of the starters has so far created more than 20 jobs (De Clercq *et al.*, 2004, pp. 28–29)."

Given the limited growth potential of a small domestic market, internationalisation is important for Belgium. The GEM report stated, "A substantial part of the Belgian and Walloon entrepreneurs have chosen to enter the international arena. Further our results suggest that the Belgian starters, on average, have a high international orientation in their business activities... However, given the overall low level of people choosing for a career as entrepreneur in Belgium, relatively few Belgian adults (1.5%) are involved in international start-up activity compared to many other EU countries. Further, we find that new ventures do not necessarily follow the classical pattern from less risky to more risky modes of foreign entry. Although export and import appear to be an important entry mode, in many cases foreign entry also involves more substantial commitments… (De Clercq *et al.*, 2004, p. 4)." The same authors elaborated, "We find that 69% of the Belgian nascent entrepreneurs were planning to enter a foreign market (De Clercq *et al.*, 2004, p. 35)." Their internationalisation discussion concluded with, "Overall, our results show that the Belgian starters, on average, have a high international orientation in terms of the location of their customers (De Clercq *et al.*, 2004, p. 40)."

3.4   *Toward the Future*

A problem revealed by the De Clercq *et al.* GEM study is that, "Belgian key informants feel that the lack of financial support is an important hindrance for entrepreneurship in Belgium (2004, p. 58)." Another problem seemed to be the fact that the Belgian educational system does

Exhibit 3.10   Youth at Marrole Festival; photo © 2005 Léo-Paul Dana

not encourage creativity, self-sufficiency and initiative. These problems should be addressed by public policy. Earlier exposure to entrepreneurship might be beneficial for the nation's youth (see Exhibit 3.10).

Entrepreneurs might benefit from tapping into existing resources. These include *UNIZO,* the Small Business Association of Self-employed Entrepreneurs, and *VIZO*, the Flemish Institute for Enterprises.

Chapter 4

Finland

4.1 *Introduction*

Finland covers 304,593 square kilometres of land, and encompasses 33,551 square kilometres of inland waters. Bounded by the Baltic Sea and its gulfs, Finland shares borders with Norway, Russia and Sweden. Graves noted, "A third of Finnish territory, the portion known as Lapland, lies almost entirely above the Arctic Circle (1968, p. 590)." (See Exhibit 4.1.) The indigenous people of the northernmost portion of this region are the Sámi people (see Exhibit 4.2).

Finland has earned first place in the Global Competitiveness Report of the World Economic Forum. Transparency International identified Finland as the country with the least amount of corruption in 2004. According to the *2005 Index of Economic Freedom* (Miles *et al.*, 2005), Finland has little regulation, low barriers, a low level of restriction on financing, a low level of intervention on prices, a very high level of protection with respect to property rights and a very low level of informal market activity. In entrepreneurial activity, however, Finland is far from first place.

Routamaa and Mäki-Tarkka stated, "The micro enterprises are of vital importance for the Finnish economy (2005, p. 114)." They added, "Relatively low motivation of Finns to start their own businesses, shortage of entrepreneurial skills, and fear of failure hinder entrepreneurial activities... Young people seem to prefer paid work instead of entrepreneurship... Also the tradition of entrepreneurship

Exhibit 4.1   The Arctic Circle Cuts through Finland; photo © 2005 Léo-Paul Dana

and natural business transfer from one generation to another is more or less missing[1] from our entrepreneurship culture (2005, p. 114)." The exception to this lies with a small minority, namely the indigenous Sámi people, who have a long tradition of passing reindeer (*Rangifer tarandus*) to their offspring (see Exhibit 4.3), thereby maintaining a spirit of self-employment.

Müller-Wille and Pelto observed occupational clustering was segmented along ethnic lines, "The Finns are mostly employed in administration, construction, and services whereas most of the Lapps still follow their traditional occupations — fishing, trapping, small farming, and reindeer herding (1971, p. 142)."

---

[1] Family Business Network (FBN) Finland arranges seminars to promote succession.

Exhibit 4.2   Sámi Entrepreneur Wearing Traditional Hat of the Four Winds; photo © 2005 Léo-Paul Dana

Although entrepreneurs in Finland are entitled to the same basic unemployment allowance as employees, Arenius *et al.* (2001) reported that Finns have little motivation to be entrepreneurs. The Global Entrepreneurship Monitor (GEM) has been central in reducing administrative barriers to entrepreneurial activity; it has also promoted entrepreneurship education. Generalising for mainstream society in Finland, Fayolle *et al.* wrote that in Finnish mainstream society, "Entrepreneurship effort is accepted, but success is not (2005, p. 23)."

Exhibit 4.3   Father and Son Team; photo © 2005 Léo-Paul Dana

In Sámi society (see Exhibit 4.4), self-employment is well looked upon and success is desirable. Many complain about changes brought about by European Union policies (Dana and Remes, 2005). Hunnisett and Pennanen explained, "While neither official Finnish nor folk attitudes towards the Saami have been particularly hostile or prejudiced, competition for resources and cultural insensitivity have gradually eroded significant portions of Saami territory, autonomy, and culture (1991, p. 212)." *While reindeer, in Finland, are individually owned, their care is a communal activity shared among entrepreneurs.* Sharing of work within the family is usually with no remuneration other than in kind; each entrepreneur is interdependent with others, in a network of symbiotic interaction. While Sámi are pulled to reindeer husbandry (see Exhibit 4.5) as means of self-employment, economic need also pushes them to work in agriculture (see Exhibit 4.6), forestry, etc.

Exhibit 4.4   Elders with a Member of the New Generation; photo © 2005 Léo-Paul Dana

Exhibit 4.5   Reindeer Husbandry is Widespread; photo © 2005 Léo-Paul Dana

Exhibit 4.6   Part-time Work on the Farm; photo © 2005 Léo-Paul Dana

4.2 *Historical Overview*

From 1155 until 1809, Finland was part of Sweden. Roma (gypsies) arrived during the 16th century (Hunnisett and Pennanen, 1991). As a consequence of the Finnish War of 1808–9, Finland became an autonomous duchy within the Russian Empire. In 1812, Helsinki (Helsingfors in Swedish) became capital of the new political entity; the city is also known as the Daughter of the Baltic (see Exhibit 4.7).

In time, Helsinki grew to be an important regional hub. A train station was built in 1914, in art nouveau style (see Exhibit 4.8) of the Finn architect Eliel Saarinen. Finland declared its independence from Russia on December 6, 1917. Finland thus became the "farthest north republic (Olson, 1938, p. 499)." Glassey described the mercantile activity at the open-air markets in Helsinki, noting that self-employed vendors were chiefly women, "While the Finns are fishing, their wives

Exhibit 4.7   Helsinki Today; photo © 2005 Léo-Paul Dana

Exhibit 4.8   Helsinki Station; photo © 2005 Léo-Paul Dana

bring the catch to the market (1925, p. 608)." Niskanen (2001) studied the role of women in the Finnish economy, finding that between the 1920s and 1950s, women on Finnish farms worked longer hours than did men.

Soviet forces attacked Finland in 1939, and in March 1940 Finland was forced to give up land to the Union of Soviet Socialist Republics. From June 1941 to September 1944, Finland fought alongside Germany against the Union of Soviet Socialist Republics. An armistice in September 1944 prompted the surrender of territory and the relocation of many Finns, including the Skolt Sámi (Ingold, 1976). Rovaniemi, the capital of Finland's Lapland province, was devastated when Nazi Germany retreated from Finland in late 1944. Bradley (1947) provided an account of post-war Finland. In 1961, Finland joined the European Free Trade Association (EFTA).

During the mid-1980s, high domestic demand led to output growth. Low interest rates during the late 1980s maintained high consumer demand. However, the boom overheated, house prices jumped and Finland found itself with a serious trade deficit. Interest rates were hiked and by 1990, local consumption was almost stagnant, trade with the Union of Soviet Socialist Republics was dwindling and unemployment was on the rise. Thus, the worst recession in several decades started in 1990 (Mahlamäki-Kultanen, 2005). Unemployment doubled in less than a year. In 1992, Finland experienced its deepest slump since World War II. Domestic demand tumbled again in 1993, before the economy began to recover in 1994. Improved competitiveness then helped exports, resulting in a current account surplus, allowing for a drop in interest rates, in turn stimulating investments, housing starts and employment.

On October 16, 1994, 56.9% of voters opted for the nation's entry into the European Union, and Finland became a full member on January 1, 1995. On February 6, 1995, Finland set up a venture capital investment company to assist entrepreneurial activities. Nonetheless, economic growth slowed in 1995. In 1996, the Foundation of Private Entrepreneurs established a fund for young entrepreneurs; an annual competition was co-organised with the Federation of Finnish Enterprises.

There has been growing interest in Finland's indigenous people. In the words of Ohlson, the Finnish "State Commission decided to include as Lapps (Sámi), those persons who spoke the Lapp language, and who had at least one parent who spoke Lapp as a native language (1960, p. 28)." Since 1996, Finland considers an individual to be Sámi if: (i) the person considers himself/herself to be Sámi, and has learned Sámi as mother-tongue; (ii) the person considers himself/herself to be Sámi, and Sámi was the first language of at least one parent or grandparent; or (iii) the parents or grandparents was recorded as a Lapp in 1932 or earlier.

4.3   *The Indigenous Sámi People of Lapland*

In former times, the Sámi people were commonly referred to as Lapps. During the 19th century, Clarke wrote, "The Laplanders, or Laps, as they are always called by the Swedes... constitute the only remaining branch of the ancient inhabitants of Finland (1824a, pp. 328–329)." Citing research conducted in Finland by Isac Fellman and Jacob Fellman, Israel Ruong provided a rich literature review (Ruong, 1937) of early studies about the Sámi people. Whitaker explained, "A Lapp was defined as a person of Lappish origin whose father or mother, or one of their parents, was a full-time reindeer breeder (1955, p. 25)." Although the Sámi are a minority in Finland, they form a majority (70%) in the municipality of Ohcejohka/Utsjoki.

Lehtola distinguished among three groups of Sámi in Finland:

> The oldest settled group are the Lake Aanaar (Anár) Sámi whose livelihood has been based on a mixed economy of freshwater fishing and small scale farming. The Deatnu Sámi have the same type of livelihood, but with the addition of reindeer herding. The Deatnu Sámi today own farmsteads and live from dairy agriculture, and raise cattle or sheep. The reindeer Sámi, who live in the regions of Eanodat, Giehtaruohtas and Soabbat, used extensive areas in the

fells until the end of the 1800s when the closing of the State borders forced them to settle in a smaller area. The Skolt Sámi today live in Čeavetjavri and Nellim (Njellin, Njeä'llem), settlements that were built after World War II for their resettlement from the Petsamo (Peäccam) area which was ceded to the Soviet Union (2002, p. 12).

With reindeer pastures comprising about 40% of Fennoscandia (Turi, 2002), the Sámi people developed a subsistence economy[2] around the domestication of reindeer (see Exhibit 4.9). Well-adapted to the harsh environment, reindeer do not require indoor feeding during the winters. The reindeer provided food and transport for the Sámi. Olson described reindeer transport, "In descending a very steep grade, the reindeer is hitched behind the sleigh. The animal resents being pulled

Exhibit 4.9   Reindeer; photo © 2005 Léo-Paul Dana

---

[2] For a discussion of subsistence self-employment, see Cole and Fayissa (1991).

by the head and digs his forefeet into the snow, thus providing effective breaks (1938, p. 512)." Fisher explained, "Here we find the usual order of things reversed, man's life being ruled by an animal's needs (1939, p. 641)."

Traditionally, reindeer herding was the dominant feature of Sámi life, and "indigenous land use was based on locally available resources (Müller-Wille, 1987, p. 352)." Until the 1940s, the Sámi people relied on local sources for their energy requirements. Given the centrality of reindeer to Sámi life, Collinder (1949) asserted the existence of thousands of words describing reindeer herding.

Whitaker noted, "The natural basic unit of Lappish society is the elementary family (1955, p. 37)." The family is in turn central to the family business. Whitaker explained, "Marriage is not undertaken until it is deemed that one has sufficient property in the form of reindeer with which to support a family. This is usually set at about 200 for the combined herd of husband and wife... (1955, p. 40)." Ruotsala explained, "Often an important factor is that this is a profession passed down from generation to the next, primarily from father to son, which is carried on in the same place as the previous generation (1999, p. 43)."

Members of one or more families co-operate in a reindeer herding working community (see Exhibit 4.10), known in Sámi language as *sii'dâ*, and the plural of which is *siidât*. Haetta wrote, "The Sami people have always had common ownership, land belonging to the group, *siida*. This is advantageous and necessary because stocks of fish, game, valuable fur animals and other resources are unevenly distributed within a district. Dividing the land into private sectors would be difficult and pointless. If land were individually owned and could be passed on to children, the size of each piece would soon become smaller and smaller from one generation to the next. Finally, individual families would not have enough land to maintain their semi-nomadic way of life (1996, p. 21)." Whitaker explained, "The individuals retain all property rights over their reindeer, and their right to leave the unit at any time (1955,

Exhibit 4.10   Part of the Herd; photo © 2005 Léo-Paul Dana

p. 54).'' The Sámi entrepreneur does not act on individualistic account, but on the account of his extended family.

Paine explained that while herding is a communal activity:

> The responsibilities of husbandry are *not* shared, they are those of the married man, and his wife, of each family herd. Married men do not interact as husbanders. Unmarried children execute the orders of their parents but do not themselves take husbandry decisions. The responsibilities of the head of the family herd are grave ones for he is not the owner of the herd but its senior custodian. The family lives off its herd and one can say they take wages from it, but the herd is also a capital asset which is re-distributed in the next generation. Thus the parent, the husbander, should each year select animals to be ear-marked in favour of each of his children (1964, p. 85).

In Finland, a local reindeer association managed either by Finnish herders or by Sámi people is called *paliskunta*. This is essentially a system of associational management among self-employed reindeer owners. As explained by Beach, "A *paliskunta* is a type of economic cooperative with a communal treasury to which members pay according to their reindeer herdings (1990, p. 277)." Lee *et al.* (2000) noted that Northern Finland contains 57 of these reindeer herding units.

In 1962, the Sámi of Utsjoki were the first in Finland to use snowmobiles in their herding. Before then, "the costs for equipment to work in reindeer herding were essentially zero… Full participation in mechanised reindeer herding, on the other hand, means cash outlays for the snowmobile (Pelto and Müller-Wille 1972/3, p. 136)." As of the 1960s, the Sámi people became increasingly dependent on imported fuel. The snowmobile revolution[3] exacerbated the situation. Paine (1994) portrayed Sámi pastoralists in the 1960s. Müller-Wille wrote, "One can refer to the modification of the reindeer economy in northern Fennoscandia with the use of the snowmobile and the motorcycle between 1962 and 1968; this meant a considerable financial outlay for the Lapp reindeer herder and led to a reindeer meat industry oriented to a market economy (1978, p. 110)." Thus, traditional subsistence herding yielded to a cash sector. Pelto and Müller-Wille observed, "The use of reindeer sleds for any sort of transportation was almost completely obsolete by 1967, and even economically marginal households throughout northern Lapland found means to purchase machines during the late 1960s (1972/3, p. 119)."

Riseth (2003) listed the regulatory principles of Sámi herding society: (i) the autonomy of the herder, in "that all husbanders are their own masters (p. 232)"; (ii) the social bonds of the extensive kinship system, resulting in "a network of mutual obligations through genetic and social kinship (p. 232)"; (iii) partnership and *sii'dâ* solidarity; (iv) dialogue and consensus; and (v) responsibility toward the land and the spirits.

---

[3] For a discussion of the snowmobile revolution, see Müller-Wille (1978).

Why have reindeer herders specialised in this occupation? One causal variable motivating Sámi people to be reindeer herders is "for the freedom (Bergsmo, 2001, p. 132)." Paine explained, "Many of the jobs of a herdsman are menial, but herding is not work of low esteem (1964, p. 84)." Unlike entrepreneurs who compete against one another in other cultural contexts, the success of each Sámi reindeer herder has traditionally been dependent on the mutual co-operation of reindeer herders.

European Union legislation, however, is changing the nature of this sector. Clarke described the traditional way by which reindeer were slaughtered, "Attended with the least pain to the animal, and the greatest profit to its possessor. They thrust a sharp-pointed knife into the back part of the head, between the horns; so as to divide the spinal marrow from the brain. The beast instantly drops, and expires without a groan or struggle, as if it fainted. The blood is not suffered to flow; but is collected afterwards into a pail from the stomach, yielding about two gallons: it is then used for food (1824b, p. 173)." No part of an animal was wasted (see Exhibit 4.11). Today, European Union legislation causes inefficiencies along with a move away from environmentally-friendly sustainability.

Jernsletten and Klokov explained, "The slaughter houses have strict regulations connected to the activity. They have to conform to the EU directives... This is creating troubles for reindeer owners trying to establish a small scale production... many of the regulations are unnecessary and only create extra costs (2002, p. 105)." Jääskö observed, "The commercialisation and centralisation of meat processing (including slaughtering) causes a decrease in numbers of people practising a reindeer economy as well as a decrease in opportunities for other local people to benefit from raw materials from reindeer. Not only does it result in reduction of jobs, but in impoverishment of the culture as well (1999, pp. 37–38)."

In the words of Riseth, "The production system changed from subsistence pastoralism to a motorised and market-oriented industry,

UNIVERSITY OF BIRMINGHAM LIBRARY

Exhibit 4.11   Reindeer Hide; photo © 2005 Léo-Paul Dana

moving away from a near-complete dependence on animal and human muscle power to a degree of dependence on motorised vehicles (2003, p. 231)." Herding activities became increasingly mechanical as the reindeer economy became a meat production business. Being more familiar with nature and their actual enterprises, than with accounting principles, Sámi entrepreneurs often complain about bookkeeping requirements imposed by their respective nation-states.

Direct dependence on nature and on the traditional family business has been reduced. Burgess (1999) found that although nobody lives exclusively from fishing, this provides a supplementary source of income and food. A problem, however, is that substantial commercial fishing has over-fished some waters. Some Sámi people must now buy fish and meat. Haetta observed, "Mechanisation and the market economy have replaced self-sufficiency (1996, p. 3)."

The traditional Sámi way of life stresses the need to live in harmony with nature, refraining from leaving physical marks on the land. As the Sámi people did not mark the territories upon which they lived, government authorities assumed that these lands were unclaimed. Consequently, non-indigenous farmers claimed land traditionally used by the Sámi people, reducing the area (see Exhibit 4.12) available for reindeer.

Although "20 females are the minimum for a practical herd (Shor and Shor, 1954, p. 269)," Lee *et al.* (2000) found that among 7,000 reindeer owners in Finland, two-thirds own fewer than 25. They explained, "Reindeer herding is an important source of income for the Saami,

Exhibit 4.12   No Longer Pasture; photo © 2005 Léo-Paul Dana

bringing in between half and three-quarters of their gross earnings. However, this income has to be supplemented by agricultural and forestry work, as well as cash-earning jobs… Although many Saami herders have additional employment, reindeer herding is still regarded as being of high cultural importance (2000, pp. 101–103)."

What can be learned from this is that the cultural values of a society determine the desirability of different forms of economic activity and the acquisition of knowledge. Entrepreneurship is then embedded in the cultural and social heritage of the society.

4.4   *The Economy, Entrepreneurship and the Small Business Sector*

Routamaa and Mäki-Tarkka wrote that the Finnish economy revolved around "forestry, metal, engineering, telecommunication and electronic industries (2005, p. 113)." As 35,000 entrepreneurs ceased operations during the recession of the 1990s, Employment and Economic Development Centres were created, and began in 1997, to support and advise SMEs. "With special reference to rural young entrepreneurship, a more active role for existing enterprises in terms of developing practical training in their home district was suggested in order to reduce migration from scattered settlements (Routamaa and Mäki-Tarkka, 2005, p. 123)."

Using a large data set from Finland, Johansson (2000) analysed the choice between being self-employed or employed. Findings suggest that "the predicted earnings differential between self-employed and paid employment has a positive influence on the probability of being self-employed in Finland (Johansson, 2000, p. 45)." Johansson elaborated, "The group of self-employed is a very heterogeneous group, ranging from successful entrepreneurs with many employees to the local pizza-maker or baby-sitter (2000, p. 53)." However, it can be said that the economy of Finland, formerly dominated by forestry, is now dominated by the high-tech sector.

As noted by Wolf-Knuts (2001), the Swedish minority in Finland was formerly very active as self-employed farmers and fishermen. As the nature of agriculture has changed, the new generation tends to choose a different sector, but self-employment is still a favoured option.

The GEM team has been active in giving importance to entrepreneurship. While self-employment and reindeer ownership is common among Sámi women, GEM research (Arenius *et al.*, 2004), showed that in Finland's mainstream society, men are more active than women in terns of start-up and in terms of new business activity.

Entrepreneurship in Finland is opportunity-driven and facilitated by a variety of institutions and schemes. At time of writing, the Entrepreneurship Policy Programme consists of five subsectors: (i) entrepreneurship education, training and advisory services; (ii) launch, growth and internationalisation of firms; (iii) taxation; (iv) regional entrepreneurship; and (v) relevant legislation.

In eastern Finland, the Small Business Centre (established by the Helsinki School of Economics and Business Administration in 1980) provides a variety of educational offerings, including a Degree for Rural Entrepreneurs. Among the research interests of the centre is the Internationalisation of SMEs.

There are 31 polytechnics operating in Finland, and each has an incubator (or equivalent). Routamaa and Mäki-Tarkka (2005) discussed the Finnish Polytechnics Incubators Network, a brain-storming community that promotes entrepreneurship.

The Inari Municipal Business Company InLike Oy Ltd has as its objective to facilitate work and subsistence in Inari for the inhabitants of this municipality. The municipality assists entrepreneurs and other economic implementing bodies with its services, co-operative network and partners to increase the economic well-being within the municipality.

Another success story in Finland is Oulu, formerly an industrial city with a heavy reliance on chemicals and pulp and paper. Today it is home to high-tech entrepreneurs (Susiluoto, 2003).

Facilitating finance, Finnvera plc provides micro-loans (up to 16,800 euro) to micro-enterprises with up to five employees. Interest rates are low and even lower for women entrepreneurs. Networks of co-ethnic immigrants also facilitate entrepreneurship.

Of course, not all entrepreneurial activity is legal. According to Lehti and Aromaa, "In addition to eastern prostitution, the Russians and Estonians, the Thai community in Finland also runs organised prostitution on a considerable scale with regard to the small size of the community... The centres of the community and its social meeting places are massage parlours, some of which also sell sex services. In addition to the Thai women permanently living in the country, the parlours also employ 'girl relatives', who visit Finland as tourists, work a three-month-period and return to Thailand (2002, p. 69)."

4.5   *Toward the Future*

GEM findings have already had a positive impact in Finland and the future appears to be bright for entrepreneurship in this country. Entrepreneurship has become one of the top priorities on the government's agenda, and it is highly emphasised in the educational system. In addition to polytechnics that offer undergraduate degrees, Finland has nine universities that teach enterprise, and most of these have specific degrees in entrepreneurship. The Turku School of Economics, the University of Kuopio and the University of Vaasa all have small business promotion centres. A network of 22 technology and science parks promotes *entrepreneurship through symbiotic networking*. Given that GEM findings suggest a relationship between entrepreneurship and a high level of education, it may be beneficial to further encourage entrepreneurship education.

A caveat, nevertheless, is that "measures aimed at increasing the number of self-employed might… increase small-scale, inefficient production leading to a decrease in social welfare… society would benefit from a greater number of high-performing, successful entrepreneurs (Johansson, 2000, p. 53)." Future research will be able to determine the level of success of recently introduced new pilot and development projects.

Chapter 5

France

5.1 *Introduction*

Neighbouring Andorra, Belgium, Germany, Italy, Luxembourg, Monaco, Spain and Switzerland, France covers 543,965 square kilometres, with distinctive regional and cultural differences. Dana (1996b) reported the findings of an empirical field study investigating a sample of 296 owner-managers engaged in micro-enterprises in Alsace; motivations for self-employment were found to vary along religious lines. (For a historical study of entrepreneurial families in Alsace, see Hau and Stoskopf, 2005.) The Basques were discussed by Laxalt (1968) and by Dana (1995b), the latter suggesting that entrepreneurs in the Basque Country are culturally predisposed toward self-employment. The Bordelais is the focus of Davenport (1980); Brittany of Walker (1965); Languedoc of Edwards (1951); the Loire of MacLeish (1966); Provence of Bryson (1995); and the Pyrenees of Laxalt (1974). The focus of Laxalt (1968) was self-employed sheep-herders in the Pyrenees. Dana (2005a) gave an account of a typical small business in the Pyrenees. (For a discussion of Basque entrepreneurs in the United States, see Laxalt, 1966). While Toulouse is home to an important aerospace industry, self-employed goat herders and shepherds form the heart of the local economy in Aregno, on the island of Corsica; Range noted that although this island was annexed by France in 1769, some residents "remain defiantly un-French (2003, p. 57)."

Among the great entrepreneurs of France were Alexandre Gustave Eiffel, André Citröen, and Louis Renault. Eiffel is well-known for the tower that he designed for the *Exposition Universelle* (World Fair) of 1889, and for the elevator that he built in Lisbon (Conger, 1948). Citröen and Renault became leading automobile manufacturers.

Today, France is considered to be a role model for its science parks and business incubators for new and growing firms. Yet, Volery and Servais' (2001) Global Entrepreneurship Monitor (GEM) study found that France displayed one of the lowest rates of entrepreneurial activity among GEM countries, and the lowest Total Entrepreneurial Activity Prevalence of all the countries in the euro-zone. France has the lowest female participation rate among GEM countries. Although French government agencies have a multitude of incentives to start new enterprises, most new firms fail. However, new ventures created by former employees of large corporations, with the help of these large corporations, are doing relatively well, and four-fifths are still in business, several years after their launch.

France is a country rich in history and in tradition, and national culture may explain the low level of entrepreneurial activity. Society, here, gives importance to the privileges of the elite; with the French Revolution, privileges of birth were eliminated, but replaced by a scholarly meritocracy. Education is valued and academics are praised. Entrepreneurs are not as valued; neither is the move to an entrepreneurial position. Yet, Ulijn and Fayolle (2004) found that France had a higher rate of self-employment than Germany or the Netherlands, and they proposed an explanation. "The low cost of setting up a business in France… might explain partly the higher percentage of self-employed (Ulijn and Fayolle, 2004, p. 211)."

5.2 *Historical Overview*

France has a long history of innovation, as well as self-employment. In 1642, Blaise Pascal made a mechanical calculator out of brass. Coquery

(1997) studied self-employed artisans of Paris in the 18th century. Musgrave (1997) examined women and guilds in Nantes, during the 18th century. The debt of France tripled between 1774 and 1789 (Severy, 1989), much of it incurred by supporting the United States in its War of Independence.

In 1789, an entrepreneur from the Cachat family began distributing mineral water from his garden; this would eventually lead to the establishment of the *Societé Anonyme des Eaux Minérales d'Evian-les-Bains*, distributors of Evian water (see Exhibit 5.1). On July 14, 1789, the Bastille — symbol of royal absolutism — was toppled.

With the fall of the Bourbon monarchy in 1792, France became a republic; the first French republic lasted until 1804 when Napoleon established his empire. In 1806, work began on the *Arc de Triomphe*, which soars 160 feet above the 12 avenues that converge at *Place de l'Etoile*. The monarchy was restored in 1814, with an interval the

Exhibit 5.1   Evian Water, First Bottled in 1826, Was Sold Exclusively in Pharmacies until 1960; photo © 2005 Léo-Paul Dana

following year. In 1820, a duty of 60% was applied to steel imports; in 1822, the duty payable on iron from England was raised to 120%. Charles X King of France and of Navarre (brother of the guillotined Louis XVI and of the post-Napoleonic King Louis XVIII) was overthrown in July 1830, and replaced by more liberal Louis Philippe. Following the 1830 revolution, the *Colonne de Juillet* was erected at the *Place de la Bastille* (see Exhibit 5.2).

In 1848, Louis Philippe abdicated and the Second Republic was established; it lasted until the Second Empire was born in 1852, under Louis Napoleon. When he was captured during the Franco-Prussian war, the Third Republic came into existence in 1870, and most of Alsace was lost to Germany. Important legislation was enacted in 1881 (see Exhibit 5.3).

The Eiffel Tower (see Exhibit 5.4) was completed in 1889. Over 900 feet in height, it remained the world's tallest structure for four decades. The turn of the century ushered in *art nouveau* architecture

Exhibit 5.2   *Colonne de Juillet, Place de la Bastille*; photo © 2005 Léo-Paul Dana

Exhibit 5.3   Important Law of 1881; photo © 2005 Léo-Paul Dana

Exhibit 5.4   *La Tour Eiffel*; photo © 2005 Léo-Paul Dana

Exhibit 5.5   *Art Nouveau* Design by Hector Guimard; photo © 2005 Léo-Paul Dana

(see Exhibit 5.5); among the most influential architects of the times was Hector Guimard whose Metro stations (see Exhibit 5.6) reflected *art nouveau*.

With the First World War, Alsace was returned to France. In 1924, art deco (see Exhibit 5.7) took the place of *art nouveau*.

In 1926, France had 20,000 immigrant business owners, of whom 7,500 were Armenians, Greeks and Jews (Mauco, 1932).

Exhibit 5.6   Metro Station Design by Hector Guimard (*Moulin Rouge* in the Background); photo © 2005 Léo-Paul Dana

Exhibit 5.7   Art Deco Style; photo © 2005 Léo-Paul Dana

Exhibit 5.8 M. Cahn Hid in the Interior, while 70,000 Jews Were Deported from France; photo © 2005 Léo-Paul Dana

Williams (1930b) gave a descriptive account of inter-war Paris. The Third Republic fell with the Nazi occupation in 1940. As Alsace-Lorraine was annexed to Germany, Jews (see Exhibit 5.8) fled for their lives. With the exception of Alsace-Lorraine and of lands ceded to Italy, occupied France was administered by the Vichy regime, a puppet government based in Vichy (see Exhibit 5.9). Walker (1940) reported about self-employed farmers in France, during World War II, and Moore (1943) provided an overview of France during the war.

As the Nazis surrendered, Alsace (see Exhibit 5.10) was returned to France. The Fourth Republic was established after the war, and Charles de Gaulle appointed Jean Monnet "to put the country back on its economic feet (Fontaine, 2000, p. 11)." Williams (1946) provided a description of post-war France.

Inspired by Jean Monnet, in 1950, the French Foreign Minister Robert Schuman made a proposal to Bonn (then capital of the Federal

Exhibit 5.9   Small Business in Vichy, Provisional Capital of France; photo © 2005 Léo-Paul Dana

Exhibit 5.10   *La Petite France*, in Strasbourg; photo © 2005 Léo-Paul Dana

Exhibit 5.11   Casablanca; photo © 2005 Léo-Paul Dana

Republic of Germany) for France and Germany to co-operate in the coal and steel industries. In 1956, France relinquished its protectorate of Morocco (see Exhibit 5.11).

In 1960, France introduced a new currency — the new franc, equal to 100 old ones. During the 1960s, the state relaxed some of its regulations (Pattisson and Lindgreen, 2004).

Exhibit 5.12   *Grands Magasins du Printemps*; photo © 2005 Léo-Paul Dana

During the 1980s, France introduced incentives to entrepreneurs in the textile industry, and leading stores (see Exhibit 5.12) promoted French clothing. The *Fonds Industriels de Modernisation* agency made available low interest loans. Subsidies were created for the acquisition of equipment, and the *Agence pour le Developpement de la Production Automatique* provided assistance for modernisation of the clothing industry. To encourage exports, additional funding was made available through the *Compagnie Française d'Assurance pour le Commerce Exterieur.* Although the larger firms were the ones who tended to criticise state intervention in the industry, these were able to benefit from schemes, more so than small-scale entrepreneurs; the smallest firms appeared to have the least time and resources to prepare a properly completed application for assistance.

Mayer (1987) observed that people were attracted to small business proprietorship, with the hope that it would help them become socially mobile. Instead of mobility, they often experienced economic hardship, and marginality, "The price of 'freedom' for small proprietors is high (Mayer, 1987, p. 56)."

The frequency of business failures in France more than doubled between 1987 and 1993, while banks were more inclined to invest in government securities rather than lend to the business sector, especially small and medium-sized firms. According to the European Observatory for Small & Medium Enterprises, small business employment growth in France from 1989 to 1993 — less than 0.5% — was among the lowest in Europe, compared to almost 4% in neighbouring Luxembourg. This should be read with caution, however, as there may be considerable under-reporting; many small-scale service providers operate in the black market, to avoid paperwork and taxation (Windebank, 1991).

Vidal (1995) demonstrated that small producers were very active in the food distribution channel in France. Paché (1996) explained that despite the marketing advantages held by larger firms, small producers may have a competitive advantage when they offer niche items that suit local preferences (see Exhibit 5.13).

Exhibit 5.13   Promoting Beer from Lorraine; photo © 2005 Léo-Paul Dana

Exhibit 5.15   Burgundy; photo © 2005 Léo-Paul Dana

Exhibit 5.16   Champagne-Ardenne; photo © 2005 Léo-Paul Dana

evolution of several regional development networks promoting small business.

The *Agence Nationale pour la Création et le Développement des Nouvelles Entreprises*, formerly referred to by the acronym ANCE, was established in 1979 to promote entrepreneurship and to observe new venture creation in each of the régions. Its name was since changed to *Agence Pour la Création d'Entreprise* (APCE). APCE conducts research, publishes guides in English as well as in French, offers specialised training courses and provides technical assistance to entrepreneurs. Across France, there are hundreds of APCE resource centres known as *Points Chances*. One out of four founders of new firms is assisted, in some way or another, by *Points Chances*; this apparently increases the probability of a venture's success by 100%.

In addition to orienting entrepreneurs, the regional representatives of APCE also function as advisers to local government. As well, the network includes *Missions Regionales à la Création d'Entreprises* (MRCE), regional missions for business creation, offering specialised expertise and policy advice.

A parallel network is that of the National Agency for Research Development,[1] known as the *Agence Nationale pour la Valorisation de la Recherche* (ANVAR). It has regional delegations ensuring the promotion of innovation and of technological development in particular. ANVAR plays a major role offering direct assistance, including financial support, management advice and technical assistance. Like ANCE, ANVAR is a public, regional development network; both are under the direction of the central government in Paris.

Yet another network, the *Agences Régionales d'Information Scientifique et Technique* (ARIST), was set up jointly by various chambers of commerce and industry and by *Chambres de Métier* (guilds and other professional associations). The objective of ARIST is to contribute to

---

[1] For a discussion, see Obrecht (2002).

the transfer of data and intelligence among small and medium-sized firms, especially where these are weak relative to larger ones. The ARIST offices, therefore, collect data, which could be of specific utility for small and medium enterprises.

Another important regional development network is the *Centres Régionaux d'Innovation et de Transfert Technologiques* (CRITT), which co-ordinates regional talent such as to adapt technological innovation to new product development and to new production processes. The *régions* have also given rise to other functional networks including incubators.

Furthermore, the *Conseils Régionaux* (local governments of the *régions*) have supported specific small business programmes at various universities. The latter, in turn, also contribute to the regional networks. The *Instituts Universitaires de Technologie* (IUT) network of technical universities offers one and two year programmes in management with an option in small business management. Also, a diploma of scientific and technical studies *(Diplome d'Etudes Universitaires Scientifiques et Techniques)* is available with a focus in small business. In Strasbourg, the Université Louis Pasteur (ULP) developed a very successful, specialised curriculum for learning about the internationalisation of small entrepreneurs. A dozen universities, across France, offer programmes in small business or entrepreneurship.

The central government has also contributed to the small business sector by relaxing regulation. Employers are no longer required to obtain government authorisation to dismiss an employee. Also helpful is that under certain conditions, an entrepreneur may be exempted for paying social security contributions for employees.

Corporate initiatives have also encouraged entrepreneurship in France. In their attempt to rationalise and become more efficient, some large corporations in France have encouraged qualified employees to quit their jobs, in order to establish independent firms, which then receive sub-contracts. Most striking is that the corporations assist their senior manager to set up the new ventures, and the new enterprise is free to provide services to other large companies, even competitors. The employee's former employer provides advice, training and networking. Forty percent of the new ventures are service firms. Major corporations involved in such schemes include: Alcatel Alsthom; the large bank, *Banque Nationale de Paris* (BNP); the power utility, *Electricité de France — Gas de France*; Hewlett-Packard; the post office, *La Poste* (see Exhibit 5.17); the car manufacturer, Renault; and Sanofi. Each of several years, 20,000 salaried employees have been giving up their jobs to become entrepreneurs with the assistance of their respective former employers. While most small businesses in France fail in their early stages, according to unpublished sources at the *Ministère des PME, du Commerce et de l'Artisanat*, the success rate of the former employees leaving their jobs to become self-employed sub-contractors is 80%, even after five years.

In addition to the networks promoting and facilitating entrepreneurship in France, there are others which assist in financing new ventures. Several foundations offer grants and/or interest-free loans. Capital may also be obtained from local financing companies, which are

Exhibit 5.17   *La Poste*; photo © 2005 Léo-Paul Dana

labelled *Sociétés de Capital Risque* (SCR). Among these are the *Sociétés de Développement Régional* (SDR), known in English as Regional Development Companies.

Depending on one's field of business and geographic location, it is also possible, sometimes, to qualify for other financial aid. The *Prime à la Creation d'Emploi d'Initiative Locale* (EIL) is a local job creation grant, while the *Prime d'Aménagement du Territoire* (PAT) is a regional development grant. The *Prime Régionale à la Création d'Entreprise* (PRCE) is a regional grant for new companies. There is also the *Prime Régionale à l'Emploi*, a regional employment grant.

Considering the availability of the above-mentioned networks of assistance, it might appear that setting up a new venture in France is relatively simple; however, the complexity of administrative formalities must not be underestimated. Paperwork must be completed at an administrative centre known as *Centre de Formalités des Entreprises* (CFE) in the district of enterprise. Once this has been done, then the applicant waits for registration to come into effect, and this may be a slow process. To expedite the process, after having completed the initial paperwork at the appropriate CFE administrative centre, it is possible to apply for a rush registration. This is done at the *Greffe du Tribunal de Commerce*. The rush procedure allows a company to be registered within five working days. With few exceptions, individuals who have not been French residents for a minimum of three uninterrupted years may not become company directors without a Commercial License for Foreigners, known as the *Carte de Commerçant Etranger*. To be self-employed, even in the arts and crafts field, one must also abide by the requirements of company directors.

Once an enterprise is created, keeping it in business is a greater challenge. There are constant paperwork requirements, numerous taxes and costly social security payments along with rigid bureaucratic procedures.

The combination of entrepreneurship promotion along with the disincentives discussed, results in significant volatility within the small and medium-sized enterprise sector. A paradox here is that while the government encourages new venture creation in France, bureaucratic regulation and taxation decrease the chances of a firm's survival. Thus, high mortality rates accompany the high birth rates. Jobs are created, but only temporarily. This is not necessarily the optimal scenario for France.

The costly access to financial markets and the lack of co-operation from the mainstream banks is also an issue. Grants are available for start-ups, but unless day-to-day banking is smooth, then periodic financial difficulties may be encountered. It would be in the mutual interest of the banks and small business, if the former would improve their attitude towards the latter. In most of Europe, the most common source of capital for new ventures is the entrepreneur himself; in France, financial institutions have been the principle source of funds. The *Fonds National de Garantie à la Création d'entreprise* (SOFARIS)[2] may provide a bank with financial guarantees. The financing of SMEs in France is the subject of Belletante *et al.* (2001).

It appears that conditions are such that many people are pushed into necessity self-employment, as opposed to being pulled toward opportunity entrepreneurship. Ma Mung and Lacroix noted that "immigrant workers, especially vulnerable to unemployment, are forced to set up their own businesses in order to survive, especially in economic sectors where sub-contracting is developing (2003, p. 187)."

5.4 *Toward the Future*

According to the state statistics bureau, between 1966 and 1998, butcher shops, cheese outlets and one-man grocery stores disappeared from half the villages (see Exhibit 5.18) of France, and the number of family-run grocery stores fell by at least 80%. Bureau statistics report that the

---

[2]SOFARIS is referred to, in English, as The National Fund for Business Loan Guarantees.

Exhibit 5.18   Self-employed Producer in Maisonsgoute; photo © 2005 Léo-Paul Dana

Exhibit 5.19   Dairy; photo © 2005 Léo-Paul Dana

number of fishmongers fell from about 4,000 in 1966, to roughly 2,000 today. Three quarters of all cheese shops have also closed down. Dairy (see Exhibit 5.19) and pastry (see Exhibit 5.20) shops have also been facing a decline.

Exhibit 5.20   Pastry Shop; photo © 2005 Léo-Paul Dana

Bureaucratic procedures and regulations appear to be a burden on the limited time and resources of owner-managers. Combined with low labour productivity, this leads to high unit costs, which in turn decreases the competitiveness of small firms.

Business start-ups (see Exhibit 5.21) are facilitated by a variety of networks and incubators, but the probability of survival is low. This is not the optimal scenario for France. The creation of a more transparent regulatory framework with simplified bureaucratic procedures would be most welcome.

Ducros *et al.* wrote, "La création d'entreprise ne se porte pas si mal en France. Mais des réformes sont encore nécessaires (2004, p. 18)." Based at EM Lyon, the GEM France has called for: more flexible labour laws; the reduction of taxes; emphasis on entrepreneurship, in the educational system; and attempts to legitimise entrepreneurship. The latter seems especially important given Fayolle's (2004) finding that, in France,

Exhibit 5.21   French-built Air France Airliner Transformed into a Restaurant; photo © 2005 Léo-Paul Dana

at a quantitative level, entrepreneurship among students and graduates was low. The economic and legislative environment often has a negative impact, and compared to other countries, entrepreneurship is more difficult in France.

Meanwhile, to overcome difficulties, small firms often find a route to success is by means of collective action. Gundolf and Jaouen (2005) found that "collective actions were allowing very small French firms to benefit from exterior resources, without loosing autonomy or making heavy capital investments."

Obrecht (2005) pointed out that the concept of "collective entrepreneurship, although new in the entrepreneurship literature, is an important feature in France, inspired by the ideology of 19th century co-operative movements in Europe. This involves entrepreneurial *individuals* who enterprise together, with common resources." He defined, "Coopératives d'Activités et d'Emploi" as "une entreprise dont les salariés sont des entrepreneurs." In other words, the workers are entrepreneurs in their own right. France has 30 such co-operatives of entrepreneurs, working under the slogan *Coopérer pour Entreprendre*. According to Obrecht, the recent success of collective entrepreneurship and its impact on decreasing unemployment are likely to lead to similar efforts beyond the borders of France. Future research might look into this.

Chapter 6

Germany

6.1 Introduction

Germany covers 356,978 square kilometres, neighbouring Austria, Belgium, the Czech Republic, Denmark, France, Luxembourg, the Netherlands, Poland and Switzerland. Among the most famous of Germany's entrepreneurs was Karl Friedrich Benz, designer and builder of the world's first practical automobile powered by an internal-combustion engine; on January 29, 1886, he received the first patent for a petrol-fueled car. His firm Benz & Company soon became the world's largest manufacturer of automobiles (see Exhibit 6.1).

Sternberg *et al.* observed, "Germany's relative strengths lie in the financing, the government programmes and political framework conditions and the status of the country's physical infrastructure (2000, p. 22)." They elaborated, "The financing of start-ups and of new, growing firms can be counted among the relatively well established framework conditions in Germany (Sternberg *et al.*, 2000, p. 23)." In their analysis, they suggested, "The number of state promotion programmes in Germany is seen as appropriate… but the experts do criticize the lack of transparency due to the large variety of programmes (Sternberg *et al.*, 2000, p. 26)."

In their 2005 Global Entrepreneurship Monitor (GEM) report, Sternberg and Lückgen (2005) confirmed that Germany's relative strengths were still in its government programmes, the political framework conditions and the national infrastructure. This time they

Exhibit 6.1   Mercedes-Benz; photo © 2005 Léo-Paul Dana

elaborated, "Germany receives best marks of all 30 GEM countries for their government programmes (Sternberg and Lückgen, 2005, p. 30)." They explained, "The number of state promotion programmes in Germany is seen as appropriate... but financing of very small new firms became more and more difficult in recent years: financing experienced the worst development of all entrepreneurial framework conditions in Germany between 2001 and 2004 (Sternberg and Lückgen, 2005, p. 27)."

There are significant demographic and regional differences in this federal republic. Jennings (1974), for instance, focused on Bavaria's regional characteristics (see Exhibit 6.2). Klandt observed that a Protestant upbringing "is more likely to lead to independent business activity than a Catholic upbringing (1987, p. 31)." Benoit (2004) and Williamson (2004) argued that important differences persisted between the east and west of this country. Benoit wrote, "It is becoming apparent

Exhibit 6.2   Traditional Bavarian Attire; photo © 2005 Léo-Paul Dana

that the two sides have begun to diverge — economically, politically and culturally (2004, p. 11)." In a more recent study, Grichnik and Hisrich (2005) explained that new ventures in the eastern *Länder*[1] of Germany were being created out of economic necessity, while entrepreneurs in the west of the country were likely to be motivated by wealth and independence; the authors suggested that people from former West Germany were relatively more entrepreneurial than Germans from the east of the country. Rocha and Sternberg confirmed, "There is a *Länder* effect on entrepreneurship (2005, p. 287)." Welter (2006) noted a lower participation of female entrepreneurs in the western *Länder*.

Comparing Germany with other countries, Ulijn and Brown noted, "The percentage of self-employed people and new start-ups in

---

[1] *Länder* is the plural of *Land*.

Germany is comparatively low compared with Japan, the USA, France and the Netherlands (2004, p. 4)." In specific, the German engineer appears to be less market oriented than the Dutch one (Ulijn and Fayolle, 2004). Groen *et al.* wrote, "To the statement: *One should not start a business if there is risk to fail…* Germans would react with 'Don't even try' (2006)." Henschel (2006) suggested that risk management, among German SMEs, is carried out in a rudimentary way, with little planning.

6.2 Historical Overview

The Germans have a rich history (see Exhibit 6.3). The guilds of medieval times established a very efficient system of local development. They established market-places, warehouses and administrative systems and thus contributed to the development of pre-industrial entrepreneurship and local trading. In his discussion of German-speaking Europe, Mumford (1938) explained that even the prostitutes formed guilds; he

Exhibit 6.3   One of Many Castles Overlooking Vineyards; photo © 2005 Léo-Paul Dana

Exhibit 6.4   Hamburg; photo © 2005 Léo-Paul Dana

noted that in Hamburg, and Augsburg, for example, the brothels were under municipal protection.

Friedrichs (1997) focused on German artisans of 17th century. Sombart wrote, "In the 17th century the importance of the Jews had grown to such an extent that they were regarded as indispensable to the growth of Hamburg's prosperity (1913, p. 20)." Hamburg prospered further with the arrival of Huguenots during the early 18th century. Exhibit 6.4 illustrates Hamburg today.

In 1791, the first Prussian-made steam engine was completed, and this paved the way for the industrial revolution that arrived during the 19th century.[2] There were political changes too, as several German states formed a union, in 1818. In 1821, Prussia created the Institute of Trades, the objective of which was to spread knowledge of new industrial methods. In 1834, a union for free trade — the *Zollverein* — was established. To facilitate transport, the railway system was developed

---

[2]See Schmidt (1999).

during the 1840s; this contributed to the development of coal-mining and industries that were made possible by coal power.

In 1866, Otto von Bismarck embarked on a mission to unify Germany. The result was the creation of a German Empire in 1871. As a result of the Franco-Prussian War, Alsace and Lorraine were awarded to Germany. The state built synagogues to attract Jews who were important entrepreneurs (see Exhibit 6.5). During the late 19th century, Italian immigrants established enterprises to import Italian goods into Germany (Wilpert, 2003).

As a result of World War I, the German monarchy was replaced by the Weimar Republic. Germany lost Alsace-Lorraine to France and part of Prussia to Poland. Germany's colonies, including South West Africa — today's Namibia[3] (see Exhibit 6.6 and Exhibit 6.7) — and Togoland[4] (see Exhibit 6.8) were taken away. The German economy suffered from the lack of natural resources, from huge payments to the Allies and from hyper-inflation. Although Sombart (1922) lauded entrepreneurs, high unemployment was inevitable. In 1933, the Nazi party rose to power, and within a few years Alsace became German again (see Exhibit 6.9).

As World War II came to a close, a black market developed and much trade took the form of barter as many people had little confidence in currency; Henry (1945) provided a contemporary account. United States military script — denominated in dollars — was used only at designated posts.

As a result of the war, the northern part of the German province of East Prussia was transferred to the Union of Soviet Socialist Republics; the provincial capital, Königsberg was renamed Kaliningrad. Alsace (see Exhibit 6.10) was returned to France.

---

[3] See Dana (1993).
[4] See Dana and Anderson (in press).

Exhibit 6.5   Balbronn Synagogue Built in 1895; photo © 2005 Léo-Paul Dana

East Germany and West Germany were founded as states in 1949. In 1954, the German Democratic Republic (East Germany) became a sovereign nation. In 1955, Federal Republic of Germany (West Germany) became its own sovereign country. While West Germany worked toward becoming a showpiece of private enterprise, East Germany became the vanguard of communism.

Exhibit 6.6   Swakopmund; photo © 2005 Léo-Paul Dana

Exhibit 6.7   Windhoek; photo © 2005 Léo-Paul Dana

Exhibit 6.8   Togoland; photo © 2005 Léo-Paul Dana

Exhibit 6.9   Strasburg; photo © 2005 Léo-Paul Dana

In West Germany, "only seven years after surrender, German factories rebuilt with U.S. Marshall Plan aid were churning out a trade surplus… The now-famous Wirtschaftswunder — the 'economic miracle' — propelled the Federal Republic into the role of Western Europe's most powerful economic force (Putman, 1977, p. 151)."

Exhibit 6.10   Return of the French Flag; photo © 2005 Léo-Paul Dana

Explanatory variables included "a remarkable political stability; a coop-erative labour movement; a social calm; the industrious German nation itself (Putman, 1977, p. 151)."

Rapid recovery, in West Germany, led to a labour shortage and series of migrations by *Gastarbeiter* (guest workers). A wave of Italians began coming in 1955, followed by Greeks and Spanish people in 1960, Turks in 1961, and Portuguese in 1964. Later, some of these would become self-employed.[5]

Meanwhile, East German entrepreneurs were banished as their estates were subdivided; the restructuring of land tenure eliminated the family farm, formerly a significant element of the small business sector. The government formally eliminated independent small business in 1972 when all small and medium-sized firms were nationalised. The number of enterprises in East Germany with 100 or fewer employees was thus reduced from almost 10,000 to fewer than 1,000. Of 855,000 farms in 1952, by 1990 only 3,850 remained.

On June 13, 1990, at Bernauerstraße, 300 East German border guards began tearing down the Berlin Wall. After 40 years of centralised

---

[5]See Fertala (2003).

planning, on July 1, 1990 a treaty on economic, monetary and social union came into effect, introducing to East Germany a social market economy — an economy based upon private ownership, competition, freedom to set prices and freedom of movement of capital, labour, goods and services. (The document regulating this reform is 243 pages long.) In accordance with Article 23 of West Germany's *Grundgesetz* (Basic Law), on October 3, 1990 East Germany was transformed into five[6] new federal states (*Bundesländer*) of the Federal Republic of Germany, already comprised of eight[7] *Bundesländer* and two city-states[8] at the time, plus West Berlin with its special status. East Berlin and West Berlin were also joined. In 1990, unified Germany represented 23% of the population of the European Economic Community.

As the poorly performing economy of the east (1989 per capita GDP was $4,500 US) was grafted to the dynamic and successful one of the West (1989 per capita GDP was $19,300 US), thousands of East German enterprises could not survive without subsidies. Unemployment in East Germany skyrocketed immediately from almost nil in June 1990 to 200,000 following unification in July (*The Economist*, July 7, 1990, p. 48) and possibly over 2,000,000 (*The Financial Post*, October 3, 1990, p. 1) after political unification in October 1990.

For entrepreneurs, however, there were countless opportunities. Small enterprises could provide employment with relatively low inputs; they could also curb existing monopolies. Indicative of an emerging entrepreneurial class in the East, 150,000 new ventures were registered during the summer of 1990. Entrepreneurs were about to be

---

[6]Brandenburg, Mecklenburg-Vorpommern (Mecklenburg-Western Pomerania), Freistaat Sachsen (the Free State of Saxony), Sachsen-Anhalt (Saxony-Anhalt) and Freistaat Thüringen (the Free State of Thuringia).

[7]Baden-Württemberg; Freistaat Bayern (the Free State of Bavaria); Hessen (Hesse); Niedersachsen (Lower Saxony); Nordrhein-Westfalen (North Rhine-Westphalia); Rheinland-Pfalz (Rhineland-Palatinate); Saarland; and Schleswig-Holstein.

[8]These were Freie Hansestadt Bremen (the Free Hanseatic City State of Bremen) and Freie und Hansestadt Hamburg (the Free and Hanseatic City of Hamburg).

Exhibit 6.11   Western Banks Assist Entrepreneurs; photo © 2005 Léo-Paul Dana

Barthian (1963; 1967) social agents of change as well as pathfinders for economic growth (see Exhibit 6.11).

Entrepreneurs from former East Germany were not alone in embarking on unprecedented opportunities. West German entrepreneurs were fast to begin their search for opportunities, and given the availability of more venture capital in the West as well as Western entrepreneurs' experience with a market-oriented economy, they had a competitive edge over their less experienced Eastern counterparts. Entrepreneurs from elsewhere in the European Economic Community also identified possibilities in former East Germany, but unfamiliarity with German language, culture and market needs increased risk and decreased the expected value of various transactions.

In the course of replacing the centrally planned economy of East Germany by one based on free market principles, 8,000 government-owned firms, formerly the backbone of East German business, were available to be privatised as of 1990. Yet, disputed property claims, poor infrastructure and low labour productivity caused big business from the West to opt against acquiring many of the state-run money-losing giants of East Germany. Western firms turned down factories which they could have obtained for free. Sources at the Berlin Economic Development Corporation indicated to the author that 70% of existing East German firms were expected to collapse. Some firms were bought and shut down.

As defunct industry needed to be replaced, the role of entrepreneurs increased, creating new ventures and jobs for former state workers. The former East German government-owned travel agency was ordered in 1990 to reduce the number of its outlets by a third; by August 1990, 2,500 entrepreneurs had applied to set up travel agencies.

By October 1990, 1,800,000 former civil servants of the former communist regime were jobless, and another 1,500,000 East Germans were working only part-time — a large pool of labour from which entrepreneurs could recruit. Self-employment and entrepreneurship were thus the optimal choice for many.

The East Germans had lived through four decades of shortages of consumer goods, while demand was high. Finally, the opportunity arose to supply such demand. There was also a tremendous demand for support services such as Western accounting previously nonexistent in East Germany. Furthermore, there was high demand for technical, management and marketing skills. East German farmers, for example, were unsure how to sell their livestock on an open market. The result was imported meat on store shelves and a surplus of local cattle in the fields.

Annexe IX of the GEMU Treaty indicates that to facilitate new venture creation, the government officially committed itself to provide "adequate property for private enterprise." Moreover, investors in former East Germany received a 12% grant from the federal government. Having achieved the world's largest trade surplus in 1989, the government could afford to pour a great deal of money into its new states, particularly into a much needed infrastructure (telephones, rails, roads, etc.), which would in turn enhance the environment for business (see Exhibit 6. 12). Meanwhile, for entrepreneurs in construction or providing infrastructure, there were tremendous opportunities.

Exhibit 6.12   The German Postal System is among the World's Best; photo © 2005 Léo-Paul Dana

Banks too were active in encouraging entrepreneurial activity. Beginning in May 1990, West German banks gave thousands of East German entrepreneurs advice on how to start a new venture. Given that post-1972 nationalisations were declared reversible, banks also offered consultations to entrepreneurs on how to buy back a family business from the state. Since unification, financial institutions have been competing to lend capital to entrepreneurs. Enhancing one's balance sheet is the fact that although savings were converted from East German *Ostmarks* to Deutsche Marks at par, the conversion rate for debits was 2:1, effectively reducing debts by 50%.

West German entrepreneurs contributed to joint ventures with East Germans, by providing market skills. On the other hand, given that in 1988, 28% of East German exports went to Eastern Europe and 37% to the Union of Soviet Socialist Republics, East German networks introduced new export opportunities for entrepreneurs from the West. German unification resulted in unprecedented opportunities for entrepreneurship.

Producers in East Germany formerly depended on subsidised pricing, without which they could not be competitive. It was no longer the case that food subsidies would allow pigs to feast on subsidised potatoes and even bread. East German manufactured goods, formerly protected by COMECON, became challenged by Western products in the marketplace (see Exhibit 6.13). Who would buy an East German television set for the price of 500 kilogrammes of beef when a superior set became available from the West at a fraction of the price?

As mentioned by Welter (2006), the 1990s saw a considerable increase in gender-specific public-private and wholly private networks for women entrepreneurs in Germany. Nevertheless, Germany experienced an overall decrease in new venture creation during the late 1990s; the trend was reversed in 2000, but business closures remained high into the 21st century.

6.3   *The Economy, Entrepreneurship & the Small Business Sector*

As Putman stated, "The Federal Republic of Germany has emerged as Western Europe's strongest, most prosperous nation (1977, p. 149)." Among the first reviews of entrepreneurship research in Germany was

Exhibit 6.13   West Germany Was the Land of Plenty; photo © 2005 Léo-Paul Dana

that by Szyperski and Klandt (1981). Schmidt (1992) examined the internationalisation of the German *Mittelstand* (SMEs). Klandt (1997) provided an update. Kontos (2003) found that between 1980 and 2000, the self-employment rate among immigrants in Germany had increased by about 30%, while the rate was 1% among Germans with local roots.

Between 1998 and 2004, the German research association *Deutsche Forschungsgemeinschaft (DFG)* funded over 20 research projects in a programme of Interdisciplinary Entrepreneurship Research. Reviewing the situation, Klandt wrote, "In spite of all the activities over the past years, entrepreneurship research in German-speaking Europe is still lagging behind (2004, p. 299)." Shortly thereafter, however, several important research studies were released, including Fritsch and Müller (2004), Sternberg and Wagner (2004), Wagner (2004), Wagner and Sternberg (2004), Rocha and Sternberg (2005), Sternberg (2005), Wagner and Sternberg (2005), Wagner (2005) and Fritsch and Schmude (forthcoming). Using Gartner's (1989) definition that entrepreneurship is the creation of new organisations, and Porter's (1988b) definition that a cluster is a geographically proximate group of interconnected firms and institutions in related industries, Rocha and Sternberg suggested that clusters added "important mechanisms to foster entrepreneurship (2005, p. 273)."

In addition to clusters, networking appears to be an important causal variable. Summarising findings from their Global Entrepreneurship Monitor study for Germany, Sternberg *et al.* wrote, "The personal and professional network around a potential start-up founder is very likely to influence the decision to launch a business. This network is primarily regional in nature. However, start-up and support frameworks vary considerably between the German regions. One reason is the federal structure, which has resulted in the development of 16 different policies for promoting start-ups at state level alone. A lack of co-ordination is obvious (2001, p. 13)." They explained, "Given the regional differences, the same business start-up programmes and techniques would have very different outcomes in different regions (Sternberg *et al.*, 2001, p. 13)." Start-up activities also vary according to sector. Lehnert (2003) noted that more new ventures were being launched in the service sector than in any other.

Ethnic minority entrepreneurship is a topic gaining significant importance, both in an economic and a political sense. The Foreigner's Law of 1965 prohibited non-Europeans from being entrepreneurs, unless they had a residence permit (Kanein and Renner, 1988). Until the 1970s, foreign labourers migrated to Germany and found employment relatively easily; self-employment was not a necessity. More recently, foreigners have been turning to self-employment in Germany. According to Wilpert, "Entrepreneurs of Greek nationality continue to have the highest self-employment rate (2003, p. 241)." According to Leicht *et al.* (2005), Austrians had the highest rate of self-employment in Germany in 2003, and in absolute terms self-employed Italians outnumbered all other ethnic minority entrepreneurs in Germany. Turkish entrepreneurs are also highly visible.

On the subject *Unternehmerin* (female entrepreneurs), Fehrenbach and Lauxen-Ulbrich (2006) noted that these tended to be in the sectors of consumer-oriented and personal services. Welter reported, "The German government only recently started paying attention to the topic of female entrepreneurship as an important means to raise the overall level of entrepreneurship... In Germany... only 6% of all women qualify as entrepreneurs (2004, p. 212)." This is less than half the proportion among men. Welter (2006) noted that compared to men, women entrepreneurs more frequently have no employees.

Worth mentioning is a special incentive for employees who choose to create their own jobs. An unemployed person may receive *Übergangsgeld* (bridging funds), along with a course — *Existenzgründer* — that includes basic law, management, advertising and taxation. Successful applicants also receive booklet of vouchers; each coupon is to be used for consultations with an accountant and a lawyer as well as a business start-up seminar.

For 60 months after becoming an entrepreneur, a former employee is entitled to receive financial benefits, as if unemployed; this reduces the risk involved in case a new venture fails within its first five years.

As stated by Bergmann and Sternberg (2005):

> Hartz IV, the reform programme focusing on the labour market and social policy in Germany at the moment, explicitly pursues the goal of bringing the unemployed to the first, or at least the second, labour market more quickly. Attempts to achieve this include push factors (cutting the level of welfare and unemployment benefits) as well as pull factors from the point of view of employers (obligation to accept very low-paid work). These measures also include instruments intended to make the step towards self-employment easier ("Me Inc." ("Ich-AG"), bridging allowances). The "Ich-AG" in particular has proved to be very popular, partly because it involves immediate financing in the form of an interest-free but limited-duration subsidy of 600 € in the first year, 360 € in the second year and 240 € in the third and last year. It is still too early to make any assessment but it is certain and plausible that these start-ups have other growth intentions and prospects than opportunity entrepreneurs. The majority of necessity entrepreneurs are primarily looking to safeguard their own living, not to generate revenue growth or additional jobs. There is no doubt that bridging allowances (more than 157,000 persons were subsidized by the end of 2003...) and the "Me Inc" have contributed to an increase of the numbers of start-ups in Germany.

6.4   *Toward the Future*

During the early 1990s, Nothdurft wrote, "Officially, Germany's export assistance programs are the territory of the private sector, particularly the chambers of industry and commerce, their overseas bilateral affiliates, the trade associations and the banking system (1992, p. 67)." Today, there is a greater interest about, and awareness of, the importance of entrepreneurs and their international activities (see Exhibit 6.14).

In a federal country, regional differences should not be ignored. As suggested by Sternberg *et al.*, "From a federal point of view, the

Exhibit 6.14   German Wines are Exported Around the World; photo © 2005 Léo-Paul Dana

emphasis should be on considering the comparative strengths of the regions and their endogenous potentials and to derive benefits from regional diversities (2001, p. 13)." Sternberg (2003) further explained that entrepreneurial activities, especially from a federal point of view, are primarily an element of *endogenous* development potential and entrepreneurial activities to promote regional development in the area of economic growth. Welter (2007) suggested that regional patterns of entrepreneurship across the East German region became increasingly distorted since the 1990s. He noted that Saxony had a high density of entrepreneurship, compared to Mecklenburg-Western Pomerania and Sachsen-Anhalt.

Chapter 7

Greece

7.1 *Introduction*

Greece, also known as the Hellenic Republic, is situated on the southern part of the Balkan Peninsula, with islands stretching into the Aegean and the Ionian. Dimitratos and Lioukas (2004) have suggested that this maritime location (see Exhibit 7.1) may have influenced the international activities of small firms in Greece. Covering an area of 131,957 square kilometres, the nation shares borders with Albania,[1] Bulgaria,[2] the Former Yugoslav Republic of Macedonia (FYROM)[3] and Turkey.[4]

Emigration from Greece during the 20th century led numerous Greek entrepreneurs to become successful entrepreneurs in Australia, Canada, New Zealand, South Africa, the United States and elsewhere. In time, family links evolved into important networks for international business. Writing about entrepreneurship in Germany, Wilpert noted, "Entrepreneurs of Greek nationality continue to have the highest self-employment rate (2003, p. 241)." While technology is exported from Greece to its neighbours, Greeks tend to prefer more lucrative trade with distant, but wealthier, business partners. The Greek merchant marine — the largest fleet in the world — constitutes about a quarter of the European Union shipping capacity. A prominent ship-owner and

---

[1] An analysis of entrepreneurship in Albania is presented in Dana (1996a; 2000a; 2005b).
[2] An analysis of entrepreneurship in Bulgaria is presented in Dana (1999a; 2005b).
[3] An analysis of entrepreneurship in the Former Yugoslav Republic of Macedonia (FYROM) is presented in Dana (1998; 2005b).
[4] An analysis of entrepreneurship in Turkey is presented in Dana (2000a).

Exhibit 7.1   A Maritime Economy Has Challenges as Well as Opportunities; photo © 2005 Léo-Paul Dana

entrepreneur of the 20th century was Aristotelis Onasis (1906–1975), international tycoon and founder of Olympic Airlines.

Greece, today, has booming financial and technology sectors. While much of the Greek economy is modern and international in nature, the government also recognises the importance of preserving the skills of traditional artisans. As noted by Koniordos, micro-firms depend "to a very substantial extent on the widespread prevalence of practices (2005, p. 167)." The handicraft and artisan sector is given special attention in Greece, and this has helped the economic development of rural areas, while avoiding uncontrolled industrialisation and urbanisation. In this way, Greece may be said to have captured the best of both worlds.

7.2   Historical Overview

In the Aegean Sea, south of the Greek mainland, lie several islands with rich traditions of trade. The Minoans had an advanced European civilisation in Crete about 4,500 years ago. These people exported wine and olives around the Mediterranean; they bought gold from Egypt and tin from Spain, and became very skilled metalworkers. Not far away, in the group of islands known as the Cyclades, the Cycladic civilisation developed between 3,000 BC and 1,000 BC. When Phoenician merchants brought papyrus from Byblos to Greece, Greek artisans began producing books. Their word for book — *biblio* — is derived from the name of Byblos, the Levantine town. Later, the English "Bible" was derived from the same.

In 166 BC, under Roman rule, the Greek island of Delos became a free port. Delos subsequently became a hub for cargoes travelling between Europe, Africa and Asia. It had a sprawling bazaar where slaves were bought and sold, as were glass, ivory, papyrus, parchment, perfumes and textiles.

Until the 15th century, the Duchy of Naxos was an important local power. Then came Ottoman rule (see Exhibit 7.2). In 1770,

Exhibit 7.2   A Remnant of the Ottomans, this *Khamissa* Was Meant to Ward Off the Evil Eye; photo © 2005 Léo-Paul Dana

Greece sided with Russia against the Ottoman Empire. In the 1821, the Greeks launched their War of Independence, and on March 10, 1829, the Protocol of London created modern Greece. When it was decided that Greece would become a monarchy, a king was brought in from Bavaria. He was forced to step down in 1862, in favour of George I of Denmark.

In 1864, Greece obtained several islands from Great Britain, including Corfu. The borders of Greece were further expanded during the Balkan Wars of 1912–1913. In 1913, Greece obtained the island of Crete, as well as fertile land of Macedonia from the Ottomans.

Between the World Wars, Williams described, "Prosaic factories now line the shore where Phryne, stepping from her garments into the sea, showed the curious populace how worthy of Prxiteles's chisel was her beauty (1930a, p. 663)." During World War II, a tomato-processing plant (see Exhibit 7.3) provided jobs on Santorini.

In 1947, Greece took control of several of the Southern Sporades, including Rhodes[5] from Italy. As a result of civil war, Greece found itself poor and unstable. This contributed to an exodus of Greeks, to Australia, Canada,[6] the United States[7] and beyond. Nevertheless, a strong work ethic helped rebuild Greece. White explained, "Between 1951 and 1971 a quarter of the work force went abroad (1980, p. 380)." Money sent home was a big factor in the Greek economy. Large Greek communities prospered in Melbourne, Australia and Montreal, Canada (see Exhibit 7.4).

In coastal areas and in the islands, fishing activities (see Exhibit 7.5) supplemented agriculture and stock-raising, the primary sources of income until the late 1950s. Sheep were important for their wool and for their meat, while goats were prized for their milk from

---

[5] For an account of Rhodes under Italian rule, see Hosmer (1941).
[6] For an account of Greek entrepreneurs in Canada, see Dana (1991).
[7] For an account of Greek entrepreneurs in the United States, see Kanellopoulos (1987).

Exhibit 7.3   Tomato-processing Factory Owned by Mr. Mindrinos; photo © 2005 Léo-Paul Dana

which feta[8] cheese was made. Not only valleys, but also hills were farmed. The cultivation of mountain slopes was made possible by the establishment of terrace farms (see Exhibit 7.6), separated from one another by low stone walls, known as *pezoules*. Mills (see Exhibit 7.7) harnessed the power of strong winds.

The military came into power in 1967, and the monarchy was abolished in 1974. A new constitution gave Greece a presidential parliamentary system in 1975. White reported that in 1977, manufacturing was

---

[8]In 1997, the European Commission ruled that the term feta is reserved for such cheese made in Greece.

Exhibit 7.4   Toula's Salon in Montreal; photo © 2005 Léo-Paul Dana

"done by firms with very few workers. In textiles, an average of thirteen; electrical appliances, eight; furniture, three (White, 1980, p. 380)." He provided data indicating that, at the time, the average number of employees per industrial firm was five. He explained, "Entrepreneurs prefer to keep down the number of permanent employees because it's hard to fire people; free-lance workers hope their arrangements will escape the tax collector (White, 1980, p. 380)."

Exhibit 7.5   Fishing Trawlers at Naoyssa; photo © 2005 Léo-Paul Dana

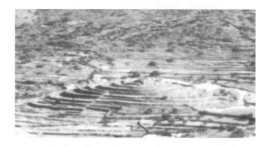

Exhibit 7.6   Terrace Farm; photo © 2005 Léo-Paul Dana

Exhibit 7.7   Remnants of Windmills; photo © 2005 Léo-Paul Dana

Exhibit 7.8   Reading about the New Europe; photo © 2005 Léo-Paul Dana

Access to the European Economic Community (EEC) accelerated economic development in Greece. White wrote, "With entry into the EEC, Greece feels pressure to improve agricultural efficiency through mechanisation. Greek farms average less than ten acres, and most are still tilled by man and animal (1980, p. 379). Greece subsequently entered the Community in 1981, and the nation soon underwent a highly intensive macroeconomic adjustment programme (see Exhibit 7.8).

7.3   *The Economy, Entrepreneurship & the Small Business Sector*

The English word "economy" comes from the Greek *oikonomos*, literally meaning "law of the house." As was the case in much of Europe, the traditional economic unit in Greece was the family firm (see Exhibit 7.9), often a family farm. The Greek Orthodox Church encouraged strong ties within the extended family, and within the community. This

Exhibit 7.9   Family Business; photo © 2005 Léo-Paul Dana

strengthened the family farm and enhanced the development of numerous family enterprises. Priests — forming a part of the extended family, and playing an important role in the community — often became involved in business.

Greek enterprises traditionally have conducted relatively little business with firms in neighbouring countries. Instead, the Greeks have focused on developing trade relations with wealthier trading partners, including Western Europeans and North Americans. About 25% of the nation's trade takes place with Germans and 10% with Italians. Also significant is the trade done between entrepreneurs in Greece and Greeks residing overseas; *such networking has led to symbiotic entrepreneurship between Greeks at home and Greeks overseas.*

In recent years, Greek banks and construction firms have been at the forefront of economic development in the Balkans. Nevertheless, parts of Greece have succeeded in retaining their romantic charm. While the infrastructure has been significantly improved since the nation's entry into the European Economic Community, caravans of mules (see Exhibit 7.10) are still used to transport goods where the terrain warrants it. On some Aegean islands, a sheer rock wall separates the harbour from the village(s). Ascension can be made by foot, but mules are the most practical means of transporting bulky and/or heavy goods. In this setting, the location of a business establishment is not strategically planned in the Western sense. Personal relationships dominate business. Since competition is limited, villagers displace themselves, to wherever the supply is being sold. In some villages, cheese is sold in a shop; elsewhere, the only place to buy cheese is at somebody's house.

Exhibit 7.10   Entrepreneur with Mules; photo © 2005 Léo-Paul Dana

Exhibit 7.11   His Father Trained Him for a Life at Sea; photo © 2005 Léo-Paul Dana

The church is central to the village and many priests are involved in business. Business partnerships often involve relatives, as the extended family is very important in Greek society. As is the case in many trades, fishing is an occupation that is often passed on from father to son (see Exhibit 7.11). However, the nature of the fishing business has been changing; Pennewiss (2004) provided an ethnographic account of the changing nature of the fishing industry (see Exhibit 7.12).

While innovative technology is playing an increasingly important role in competitiveness, a priority in Greece has been, and continues to be, the encouragement of artisans to maintain their handicraft activities. The Development Centre of Arts and Crafts (KEBA), and the National Organisation of Greek Handicrafts (EOEX), were both pioneers in promoting the handicraft activities of artisans in Greece. Today, the principal body doing this is the Hellenic Organisation for Medium and Small-Size Enterprises and Handicrafts (EOMMEX).[9]

---

[9]For a detailed discussion of the Hellenic Organisation for Medium and Small-Size Enterprises and Handicrafts, see Dana (1999d).

Exhibit 7.12　Egyptian Employees Working for Greek Fisherman; photo © 2005 Léo-Paul Dana

EOMMEX is a non-profit organisation was established in 1977 by Law N°707, under the supervision of the Ministry of Industry, Research, Technology and Trade. Funded by the European Union as well as by the national government, EOMMEX is responsible for maintaining a favourable environment for entrepreneurship development. The organisation lobbies to enhance the economic climate for small enterprises. Also, EOMMEX trains entrepreneurs and provides them with financial assistance and marketing services.

EOMMEX focuses special efforts to encourage the handicraft and arts-and-crafts sectors. It provides artistic and technical assistance, in addition to marketing services. Specific projects focus on ceramics, costume jewellery, knitting, lace, sculpturing and even the building of sea vessels.

The EOMMEX Training Department organises seminars and field visits, during which artistic and technical advice is provided.

The Technical Assistance Department is available for consultation with respect to location selection and infrastructure support; it also assists with applications for grants. The Marketing Department conducts market research and trains artisans in the commercialisation of handicrafts. Artisans are encouraged to participate in commercial fairs. Offices in Frankfurt and in New York help with the international marketing of crafts. Furthermore, an EOMMEX matchmaking service links Greek artisans with import houses overseas.

Also, there is a special programme for handicraft development in rural areas. Thus, EOMMEX has been contributing to a healthy handicraft sector throughout Greece. The organisation's activities have been enhancing job satisfaction, as well as profitability, in rural areas. This makes it possible to curb urbanisation, while preserving culture and assuring a bright economic future.

In coastal areas, tourism has led to economic and social transformation, with considerable opportunities for entrepreneurs. Barth (1963; 1967) explained how entrepreneurs can become agents of social change. In Greece, tourism led entrepreneurs to transform the economy of some regions. Although merchants had traditionally used a cost-plus method of pricing, it became more interesting to charge the highest prices that the market could bear — and tourists were willing to pay inflated prices. Dana (1999e) analysed change on the island of Ios, one of the Cyclades (see Exhibit 7.13).

During the initial stages of economic change, only a few entrepreneurs internalised the cognitive and normative themes intrinsic to the evolving environment. A variety of causal variables may explain why these individuals were open to change. Some people, with entrepreneurial personalities, may have resented conforming to established norms. Others may have been maladjusted to the traditional status quo. By internalising new economic structures, they prospered.

Dimitratos and Lioukas (2004) examined independent Greek firms, which employed between 10 and 250 employees; this study

Exhibit 7.13   Ios; photo © 2005 Léo-Paul Dana

revealed that Greek respondents considered aspects of their own culture, norms and mentality to be more similar to those of neighbouring Balkan countries, than to those of their partners in the European
Union. The study also reported that Greek entrepreneurs have recently
been launching business ventures in neighbouring Balkan nations with
emerging markets. In addition, a content analysis suggested that respondents hoped for the establishment of foreign direct investment, at a later
stage. In other words, internationalisation would take place incremen-
tally. Despite recent opportunities in international entrepreneurship,
the authors noted the following:

> The average Greek firm is tiny in the foreign markets according
> to international standards, and went abroad lately... Most Greek
> firms still emphasise operations in their domestic market and view
> foreign markets as secondary to their targets and goals (Dimitratos
> and Lioukas, 2004, p. 468).

7.4 *Toward the Future*

Greece has evolved from a poor country 50 years ago to a modern economy set for the future. Furthermore, assistance from the European Union has greatly accelerated the economic development of Greece.

While gaining from the experience of others, Greece is being careful not to repeat errors already made elsewhere. While other countries have been suffering the effects of rapid urbanisation, Greece has recognised the advantage of keeping rural people in the countryside. To this end, the state assists rural artisans, thereby contributing to regional development and social stability.

Chapter 8

Ireland

8.1 *Introduction*

The Republic of Ireland, the Celtic Tiger, covers 70,283 square kilometres. It neighbours Northern Ireland, which is part of the entity called the United Kingdom of Great Britain and Northern Ireland. The Republic of Ireland has two official languages, Irish (see Exhibit 8.1) and English.

The Global Entrepreneurship Monitor (GEM) found Ireland to have the highest Total Entrepreneurship Activity (TEA) of any non-Nordic country in Europe. Some of the entrepreneurial activity has been facilitated by foreign multinationals. While the state has a high TEA rate, it is highly dependent on foreign multinationals, which in the 1980s and 1990s were attracted by low wage rate, a skilled English speaking workforce and low corporation tax rates. The state's economy is particularly open. In 2002, 79.33% of the sales from agency-supported firms in manufacturing and internationally trade services were exported. Foreign-owned firms had a higher rate of 92.43% compared to only 37.24% for indigenous enterprises. Foreign-owned enterprises accounted for 76.26% of sales (Enterprise Strategy Group, 2004). These figures illustrate the relatively poor performance of the indigenous sector (see Exhibit 8.2). The Enterprise Strategy Group also warned against falling competitiveness, and highlighted the increased importance of developing indigenous enterprise.

Exhibit 8.1   Road-sign; photo © 2005 Léo-Paul Dana

Exhibit 8.2   Not Concerned with Growth; photo © 2005 Léo-Paul Dana

8.2   *Historical Overview*

Ireland was ruled by London (see Exhibit 8.3) until the first half of the 20th century. The Irish Free State was proclaimed in April 1916, and reaffirmed in January 1919. In December 1921, a treaty was signed whereby Ireland accepted dominion status subject to the right of Northern Ireland to remain under British rule. The Irish Free State thus became a dominion in 1922. In December 1925, a border was agreed to whereby six of the counties of Ulster were in Northern Ireland, and the remaining 26 counties (see Exhibit 8.4) were in the Free State. Starting in 1928, the Irish pound was at par with the Sterling. Until 1931, the State had a *laissez-faire*, non-interventionist policy for business. In 1932, the state attempted to encourage manufacturing (see Exhibit 8.5) in Ireland, through protectionism (see Exhibit 8.6).

Exhibit 8.3   Royal Mail Box from Queen Victoria's Time; photo © 2005 Léo-Paul Dana

Exhibit 8.4   Traditional Thatched-roof Cottage; photo © 2005 Léo-Paul Dana

Exhibit 8.5   Local Manufacturing Enabled Import Substitution; photo © 2005 Léo-Paul Dana

Exhibit 8.6   Customs House, Dublin; photo © 2005 Léo-Paul Dana

The Republic of Ireland was proclaimed in 1949. About the new republic, Sheats wrote, "There is no industry[1] (1951, p. 657)." Until 1970, most of Ireland's exports were agricultural (Scofield, 1969). Ireland joined the European Economic Community in 1973, and pursued a policy of rapid industrialisation (Exhibit 8.7). Until 1979, the Irish pound remained at par with the Sterling; following Ireland's adherence to the European Monetary System, this was no longer the case.

Putman (1981) noticed growing prosperity in Ireland. Yet, entrepreneurship did not thrive. El-Namaki (1992) noted that propensity to enterprise in Ireland decreased between 1971 and 1975, dropping further by 1981, and even lower by 1985. As unemployment peaked at 17.8% in 1986, the Industrial Development Act recognised the need to encourage the small enterprise sector.

---

[1] Burke (1995) aimed at explaining industrial development in Ireland.

Exhibit 8.7   Cork; photo © 2005 Léo-Paul Dana

Simultaneously, the concept of technology parks was tested. Abetti *et al.* (1987) described key factors influencing the location decision process of new entrepreneurial firms at Ireland's Plassey Technology Park, adjoining the National Institute of Higher Education of Limerick (now the University of Limerick), close to Shannon Airport where the first duty free shop in the world was established as part of the Shannon Free Area Development Company.

Until the 1980s, sheep (see Exhibit 8.8) and dairy cattle (see Exhibit 8.9) were very important for the economy. During the following decade, Conniff (1994) noted that manufacturing surpassed farming in Ireland. Walsh and Anderson found that, "Irish entrepreneurs who start a business are not as innovative in their decision-making preference as are U.S. entrepreneurs (1995, p. 5)." This is echoed by the low level of investment in Research and Development which still pertains in Ireland (Enterprise Strategy Group, 2004).

Exhibit 8.8   Sheep; photo © 2005 Léo-Paul Dana

Exhibit 8.9   Three-month-old Fresian-Holstein Bull; photo © 2005 Léo-Paul Dana

Exhibit 8.10   Adapting to Changing Times; photo © 2005 Léo-Paul Dana

In May 2005, the Minister for Enterprise, Trade & Employment launched a new strategy for Enterprise Ireland. With the theme of transforming Irish industry (see Exhibit 8.10), this focused on accelerating the development and internationalisation of Irish-owned firms.

8.3   *The Economy, Entrepreneurship & the Small Business Sector*

Up to the 1980s Ireland's economic strategy was heavily focused on foreign direct investment and this investment is largely responsible for the Celtic Tiger. It was the Telesis Report of 1982 and the Culliton Report of 1992 which led the shift to more attention being paid to indigenous enterprise.[2] Many of the recommendations of the subsequent Task Force on Small Business were implemented and local enterprise support was provided through the establishment of County Enterprise Boards in each county, aimed at supporting small scale- and micro-enterprises. At the other end of the scale, Enterprise Ireland supported high-potential start-ups and the export activities of established enterprises (Ní Bhrádaigh, in press).

At present, Ireland is highly supportive of SMEs, providing accelerated depreciation, cost-free advice, grants, interest allowance, interest subsidies, social security concessions, soft loans, tax concessions, tax relief for exports and training. The Accelerated Export Development Programme assists SMEs to accelerate exports. Area Based Partnerships (ABPs) provide access to networks, booking service, business advice, grants, incubators, legal assistance, loan guarantees, revolving loans, secretarial service and training. Business Innovation Centres help entrepreneurs to network and thus internationalise. The ABPs are largely about community development and the social economy.

Business Innovation Centres also help entrepreneurs network (see Exhibit 8.11) and internationalise. *Networking results in a symbiosis, making the group stronger that the sum of its constituents.* The Fusion Programme of Inter*Trade*Ireland encourages co-operation between Northern Ireland and the Republic. LEADER, an initiative funded by the European Union, provides grants to stimulate innovation in the rural sector. Shannon Development (formerly the Shannon Free Airport Development Company) provides grants and mentoring in the mid-west region. The state's Small Business & Local Enterprise Unit formulates policy proposals. *Údarás na Gaeltachta* (The Gaeltacht Authority) provides grants and equity in Irish-speaking areas.

---

[2] For a detailed discussion of indigenous entrepreneurship in the (Irish speaking) Gaeltachtaí of Ireland, see Ní Bhrádaigh (in press).

Exhibit 8.11   Networking Has Shifted Away from Pubs; photo © 2005 Léo-Paul Dana

As discussed by Bell *et al.* (2004), initiatives include guidance on addressing financial, human, and managerial resource gaps, assistance in developing international market research skills, encouraging technology transfer from academia to industry and the support of management development. *Facilitating the development of networks is also a common feature of programmes, and these networks are crucial to improving the international competitiveness and performance of entrepreneurs and their SMEs.*

A problem, however, is that there are perhaps too many facilities with overlapping services and a gap between the services provided by the Country Enterprise Boards and those provided by Enterprise Ireland. A rationalisation may be beneficial, as efficiency would be increased by streamlining.

Ireland has been involved in the GEM studies since 2000. The research has highlighted the shortage of seed capital, and the relatively low proportion of women entrepreneurs. The Irish GEM report stated, "The rate of participation by Irish women in entrepreneurial activity halved between 2001 and 2003 (Fitzsimons and O'Gorman, 2004, p. 2)." Fitzsimons and O'Gorman elaborated, "The ratio of female to male entrepreneurs in Ireland is much lower than it is in Europe (2004, p. 5)."

The Irish GEM found that entrepreneurs tend to be well-educated men in their mid-thirties, slightly older than in other participating countries. Entrepreneurship in Ireland is opportunity driven, mostly in the service sector. "The majority of the business ideas being exploited are not characterised by significant innovation (Fitzsimons and O'Gorman, 2004, p. 19)." Gibbons and O'Connor (2005) found that entrepreneurial SMEs in Ireland tended to adopt more formal strategic planning approaches than conservative firms that relied on incremental approaches.

8.4   *Toward the Future*

Ireland has a culture supportive of entrepreneurial spirit. Yet, Fitzsimons and O'Gorman warned, "There is no cause for complacency, however, as there are some worrying indicators mixed in with the good news that might suggest a decline in activity in the years ahead… Moreover, the experts and entrepreneurs, consulted as part of this research, point to a number of serious limitations that inhibit the full realisation of the entrepreneurial potential within Ireland. At the same time, recognition of good opportunities for new businesses among the general public is decreasing… (2004, p. 49)." These concerns are echoed in the Enterprise Strategy Group's report of 2004.

Thanks to multinational corporations, Ireland's exports have been very high. In fact, Ireland is the world's largest exporter of Viagra. However, there is a risk inherent in an economy being largely dependent (see Exhibit 8.12) on a small number of large multinationals, such as HP, IBM, Intel, Microsoft and Pfizer.

Fitzsimons and O'Gorman's GEM report includes the following recommendations: "Enterprise Ireland must reduce its bureaucracy, improve the speed of its decision making and its delivery of services

Exhibit 8.12   "What if They Pull Out?"; photo © 2005 Léo-Paul Dana

to clients. Enterprise Ireland should confine its VC activity to areas where there is real market failure, i.e., early stage and in the area of business angels. Enterprise Ireland must become a deeper knowledge resource for potential entrepreneurs and new companies. The resources of Enterprise Ireland should be made available to a broader group of new and potential entrepreneurs than at present... Young companies should be given access to international marketing mentors, relevant and experienced executive directors and to entrepreneurs who have experience of starting and growing a successful business (2004, p. 51)." Again, the Enterprise Strategy Group makes the same recommendations.

In addition, it was suggested to expose all students to the possibility of an entrepreneurial career, and to equip them with relevant skills. Experts interviewed for the GEM report suggested the following: "Integration of the concept of enterprise into all levels of the education system. Increasing linkages between industry and the education system at all levels. Reviewing the education system to ensure that it is delivering appropriate skills, such as independence and innovation (Fitzsimons and O'Gorman, 2004, p. 53)." The authors of the GEM report added, "A way needs to be found to identify the most appropriate delivery mechanism to fill the management gap that currently exists among entrepreneurs. This may take the form of mentoring or training (Fitzsimons and O'Gorman, 2004, p. 54)."

Chapter 9

Italy

9.1 *Introduction*

Italy covers 301,308 square kilometres, neighbouring Austria, France, Monaco, Slovenia[1] and Switzerland. Italian territory enclaves two different states, i.e., San Marino and the Vatican. Rome serves as the capital of the Vatican, as well as the national capital of Italy.

As recently as the 1970s, the Italian government did not foster SMEs, but it was lax in extracting tax[2] from owner managers (Bagnasco and Messori, 1975). Until the mid-1980s, the concept of entrepreneurship enjoyed very little popularity in Italy. Amatori and Colli wrote, "To the most important ideologies which dominated the intellectual climate — Catholic, Marxist, Idealistic — 'entrepreneur' appeared a minor if not negative, characteristic of the national scenario. He or she was often blamed as a 'freeloader' of public resources, an exploiter of workers, a fiscal evader — essentially a social actor inclined to violate common rules of society in favor of self-interest (2004, p. 243)."

Italy has important regional differences, with latitudinal variations in attitude and lifestyles, as well as climatic differences; even architecture varies, reflecting historical and economic factors (see Exhibits 9.1, 9.2, and 9.3). In their Global Entrepreneurship Monitor (GEM) study,

---

[1] For a discussion of entrepreneurship and SMEs in Slovenia, see Dana (2005b).
[2] A generation later, Smiley wrote, "A good fifth of the tax due, it is generally reckoned, remains uncollected (2001, p. 13)."

Exhibit 9.1   Rich in History; photo © 2005 Léo-Paul Dana

Minniti and Venurelli (2000) noted that while there are substantial differences between regions,[3] the Italian economy is in general characterised by a large number of micro-firms, which create jobs and contribute to GNP. Magatti (2003) noted that Italy has a higher concentration of micro-firms than is the case in most of Western Europe. Explanatory variables appear to include the crafts tradition, the importance of the family, and Mediterranean individualism.

"In addition to self-employment (involving an activity where there are no employees involved), a major component of the Italy economy consists of millions of micro-firms... They constitute an essential component of the Italian economy as well as Italian society. Their presence is stronger in the north and centre of Italy than in the south

---

[3]In recent years, the SviluppoItalia Agency for Economic and Entrepreneurial Development has helped the south develop faster than the already-advanced north.

Exhibit 9.2   Pisa; photo © 2005 Léo-Paul Dana

Exhibit 9.3   Naples; photo © 2005 Léo-Paul Dana

(Magatti, 2003, p. 163)." Minniti (2005), however, suggested a possible shift in the economic landscape of Italy as she found that people in the south are more likely to launch a new venture, than those in the north; this may be due to Law 44/86, which provides support to young entrepreneurs in the south (Maggioni *et al.*, 1999). Further evaluating the effectiveness of this law, Del Monte and Scalera (2001) found that assisted firms had higher survival rates than spontaneous rates.

Nowadays, entrepreneurial spirit is encouraged in Italy and the attitude toward entrepreneurship is somewhat favourable (Minniti, 2005). Among Italy's famous entrepreneurs are Giorgio Armani[4] and Silvio Belusconi.[5] Italy is a world leader in fashion (see Exhibit 9.4).

Exhibit 9.4   Advert; photo © 2005 Léo-Paul Dana

---

[4] See Ellis (1984).
[5] See McCarry (1992).

9.2 *Historical Overview*

Bamford (1987) suggested that SMEs in Italy are strongly shaped by historical factors, and Italy has had a rich history, with regional events shaping various regions.[6] Genoa (see Exhibit 9.5) and Venice (see Exhibit 9.6) were once great maritime powers on their own right. By identifying oneself as Romano (a citizen of Rome), Palermitano (from Palermo) or Fiorentino (Florentine), one expresses a unique cultural identity; in fact, *some people strive to build a unique difference.*

Exhibit 9.5   Genoa; photo © 2005 Léo-Paul Dana

---

[6]For a specific discussion about Capri, see Mitchell (1970); Bianchi (1990) focused on Tuscany; Judge (1972) focused on Venice; Zwingle (1995) discussed artisan glassmakers in Venice. Porter (1990) examined the ceramics sector in Sassoulo. Bianchi compared regions in Italy, noting that the Centre-North-East, "despite the absence of standard prerequisites for development, was growing faster than the old industrialized regions in the north (Piedmont, Lombardy), while those regions of the south (the 'Mezzogiorno') that received massive public investment refused to adapt (1998, p. 94)."

Exhibit 9.6   Venice; photo © 2005 Léo-Paul Dana

In 1797, the last doge of Venice surrendered to Napoleon, bringing to an end the 1,100 year old Venetian Republic. The Kingdom of Italy was proclaimed in 1861, and the country expanded in 1870. In 1912, during the Italo-Turkish War, Italy occupied Rhodes and other Dodecanese Islands. Until 1936, Italy's colonial possessions were Tientsin (in China) and Eritrea, Libya and Somaliland, in Africa; that year Italy took over Abyssinia (Stamp, 1939). Italian is still spoken among some people in Ethiopia (see Exhibit 9.7).

During World War II, gasoline was rationed and motor vehicles were converted to use charcoal (Patric, 1940). In her account of wartime Rhodes and the neighbouring islands also occupied by Italy since 1912, Hosmer noted occupational clustering, "The Orthodox population lives chiefly from the sea… while the Jewish population busied itself with commerce… The Mussulmans, aloof and conservative, live almost entirely from the land (1941, p. 449)."

On June 10, 1946, Italy became a republic, ending the reign of the House of Savoy, kings of Piedmont for nine centuries, and kings of

Exhibit 9.7   In Ethiopia; photo © 2005 Léo-Paul Dana

Italy since 1861. Hume (1949; 1951) and Hutchison (1951) provided accounts of post-war Italy.

In 1955, Italy agreed with Belgium, France, Germany, Luxembourg and the Netherlands to strive toward economic integration, and this led to the signing of the Treaty of Rome in March 1957.

Walker (1963) discussed self-employed Italian artisans, farmers, fishermen and winemakers (see Exhibit 9.8) during the early 1960s. The 1970s brought economic malaise, "During the Seventies Italy appeared on the verge of total collapse. Inflation post oil shock approached 20%, official unemployment 8% (Amatori and Colli, 2004, p. 251)." Large firms began sub-contracting an increasing amount to SMEs and, as noted by Luciani, "the number of small firms in Italy employing fewer

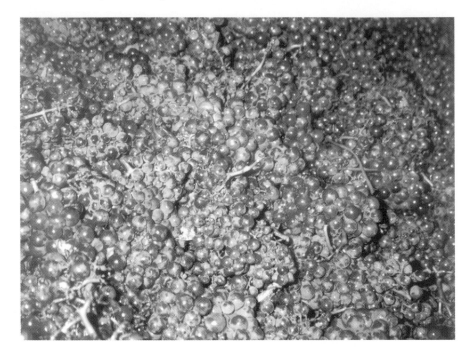

Exhibit 9.8   Italy Has Lush Grapes; photo © 2005 Léo-Paul Dana

than 100 workers increased by 21% over the 1970s compared to just 4% in the 1960s (1987, p. 35)." He added, "The number of industrial firms in Italy rose from 650,000 in 1971 to 958,000 in 1981, as masses of Italian workers left their employers to start their own small workshops and factories (Luciani, 1987, p. 35)."

Describing Italy during the 1980s, Ellis noted, "There are tens of thousands of small and medium-size manufacturing companies throughout the country today, and they are the sprinters in the race against crushing recession. In many cases, employees of a company all belong to a single family (1984, p. 193)." Comparing firms in the Federal Republic of Germany with those in Italy, he pointed out that "the average Italian company has 14 workers as compared with... West Germany's 80 (Ellis, 1984, p. 193)."

Luciani also provided comparative statistics, "Firms with fewer than 100 workers employ 51% of the Italian production workforce vs. 29% in West Germany, 17% in Britain and 25% in France (1987, p. 35)." McCarry observed, "In 1986 the country's gross national product surpassed that of Britain, making it the fifth largest economy in the world, after the US, Japan, Germany and France. To a large extent Milan was the locomotive of this success. Milan alone accounts for 10% of Italy's GNP, has 38% higher per capita than the rest of Italy, and pays 25% of the nation's taxes (1992, p. 94)." Milan also accounts for considerable consumer spending (see Exhibit 9.9).

On the eve of the 1990s, Bianchi noted, "In Italy 99 out of 100 enterprises (of all sectors: agriculture, industry, tertiary sector) are Small/Medium Sized Enterprises (SMEs), with less than 50 employees; 62 out of every 100 workers are employed in a SME (1990, p. 57)." He concluded that the state was not doing enough for the SME sector and that policies targeted for SMEs were making a negligible contribution to the sector in terms of technological enhancement and competitiveness. Nevertheless, *intense co-operation among SMEs* helped them compete successfully with vertically integrated large firms (Beccatini, 1990).

Grimond wrote, "Hardly any Italians can really bring themselves to believe in privatisation (1990, p. 13)." Italy launched its programme of privatisation in 1993. The new millennium ushered in a variety of incentives and tax reliefs to SMEs in Italy. Tax credits were introduced for the purchase of machinery and subsidies for employee training programmes. Yet, much employment continued to be unofficial. McDonald *et al.* noted, "Small and medium-sized companies in Italy, particularly where they are owned by the management of the company, are thought to be extensively involved in black economy activities (1994, p. 49)." More recently, Cockburn reported, "Among the estimated 60,000 Chinese now living in Italy, legal and illegal immigrants have been found labouring side by side with slaves (2003, p. 12)."

Exhibit 9.9   Milan; photo © 2005 Léo-Paul Dana

Magatti and Quassoli (forthcoming) observed a Chinese ethnic enclave in Milan, and compared this with Egyptian entrepreneurs in Italy. They found that while Chinese entrepreneurs were being trained by other Chinese, the Egyptians were acquiring skills from Italians.

Peet (2005) noted that the Italian industry was highly vulnerable to Asian competition. In 2005, the Italian economy dipped into recession.

9.3   *The Economy, Entrepreneurship & the Small Business Sector*

Weber wrote, "As every employer knows, the lack of *coscienziosità* of the labourers of... Italy as compared with Germany, has been, and to a certain extent still is, one of the principal obstacles to their capitalistic development (1930, p. 57)." Yet, *Italian family businesses[7] have been central to economic development.*

Italians feel more loyal to the family than to the firm or to the state. Ellis noted, "For the average Italian the first loyalty is to family (1984, p. 185)." Luciani observed, "To prosper, many Italian firms depend on family financing (1987, p. 34)." McCarry explained, "Unlike those in most industrialised nations, in Italy about four-fifths of private companies are small businesses, the vast majority family owned (1992, p. 98)." Blim (1992) showed how *kin networks* were important in generating labour and capital in the launch of small-scale industry in Italy. Smiley reported, "The bonds of family, which elsewhere in Europe are getting weaker, in Italy seem pretty sturdy (2001, p. 3)."

Some firms are registered in the name of mothers or wives, in order to take advantage of special tax laws and programmes that favour female ownership (Minniti, 2005). This is perhaps why Capaldo (1997) found that female entrepreneurship is widespread in Italy.

Bianchi (1998) noted that production, in Italy, tended to possess — among other characteristics — the following: labour intensiveness; flexibility; elasticity; and technologically divisibility. Examining the agglomeration of enterprises, Bianchi (1998) observed non-competitive relationships and emphasised the importance of the family.

More recently, Magatti listed reasons for the strength of self-employment and small firms in Italy, "The artisan tradition so strong in many Italian regions, the role of the family as an economic unit, the

---

[7] For a discussion of family businesses in Italy, see Shor (1968).

tacit pact between the *ceti medi* (middle class) and the political power since 1945, the weakness of large Italian corporations, the deep-seated inclination toward autonomous initiative and the existence of a cooperative climate in many localities, the possibility of social mobility made available by autonomous activities, the high level of unemployment and rapid industrial organisation which encouraged redundant workers to find alternative employment, and strategies followed by many firms towards externalisation. These important factors all served to reinforce this sector in Italy (2003, p. 163)." The banking and finance system followed a similar path (see Exhibit 9.10).

Harrison (1992) discussed the existence of a cooperative climate in Italian industrial districts, adding to Brusco's (1986) study of industrial districts in Italy, and contributing to the canonical district model. The model essentially emphasised: "(1) spatially concentrated and sectorally specialised small and medium-sized producers; (2) intensive vertical and

Exhibit 9.10   *Credito Italiano*; photo © 2005 Léo-Paul Dana

horizontal inter-firm linkages, consisting of market and non-market exchanges of goods, information, services and people, within a deep and localised social division of labour; (3) a common social and cultural background that connects economic actors and provides a common code of behaviour; and (4) supportive public and private institutions (Rama *et al.*, 2003, p. 73)." Rabellotti (1995) also focused on industrial districts, and compared footwear districts in Italy and Mexico. A comprehensive collection on this subject is Becattini *et al.* (2003), and a more recent contribution is Becattini (2004).

Comparing Italy with other countries, Kantis (2005) found that entrepreneurs in Italy were more likely to have had self-employed parents, than was the case elsewhere. He found that role models were not a very important factor in Italy, but that family influence perpetuated the tradition of being in business; he noted that this tradition was more prominent here than in East Asia, Latin America and Spain. He also mentioned the high interrelationship existing in Italian industrial districts between the different spheres where, for example, there is great deal of overlap between business and family.

About families in the shadow economy, Ellis wrote, "Behind the familiar trademarks of Italy's official marketplace has emerged a dynamic 'shadow economy' of unreported wages and profits. Producing a cornucopia of leather goods, textiles, furniture, and other products, tens of thousands of family workshops add perhaps 15% to 20% to the nation's GDP (1984, p. 187)." He elaborated with the comments of an interviewee: "According to the figures, we have high unemployment in Naples… But the figures are misleading. Many people are on the unemployment list, but not all of them are telling the truth. They are working… for friends and cousins (1984, p. 192)."

Ellis quoted professor of economics Bruno Contini of the University of Turin, "I would estimate that the people included in the underground economy account for about 20% of the work force in Italy… These economic activities are not necessarily illegal, but in most cases they do violate certain existing government regulations, both for tax evasion purposes and for the purposes of evading legislation having to do with labour protection (1984, p. 193)." Magatti confirmed, "The Italian informal economy is rather large, especially in the south where, according to some scholars, a quarter of all employment is irregular (2003, p. 158)."

Law 266 of November 22, 2002 attempted to make SMEs emerge from the underground economy by reducing their fiscal burden. However, only 632 emerged, with a total of 2,216 workers. (According to the World Bank, the informal economy represented 27% of the gross national income in Italy in 2004.)

Magatti observed that "self-employment is mainly prevalent in the most advanced and dynamic Italian regions (Emilia Romagna, Lombardy, Veneto, etc.), and that in the Italian social hierarchy, self-employment offers good opportunities for social mobility, which can be taken even by people without a formal education (2003, p. 163)." This is consistent with earlier findings by Dana (1992b), who concluded that in Italy the most significant training of entrepreneurs appears to be the marketplace, as opposed to academic institutions. Entrepreneurial skills are developed through practice, with concrete experience leads to observations and reflections which are used to form abstract concepts, the implications of which are eventually tested in new situations, setting the ground for more concrete experience which again becomes the basis for further learning.

Learning through networking can be an effective substitute for academic credentials. Kantis (2005) found that only one in four entrepreneurs in Italy was a university graduate, less than half the rate in the other countries. He suggested that this shows that technical knowledge circulates through broader channels than those provided by institutions of higher learning. In Italian industrial districts, networks of SMEs are channels of knowledge. This builds on the findings of Bagnasco and Messori (1975), who noted that Italian firms had developed complex networks of reciprocal relationships amongst themselves. This often involves specialisation made possible by the division of labour among firms. These networks result in economies of scale external to each individual entrepreneur, but internal to the network.

Networks also provide entrepreneurs in Italy with access to funding resources. Kantis (2005) found that in contrast to Latin America, where the main reason offered to explain the non-use of outside sources of finance was the lack of an appropriate supply, 86% of respondents on Italy stated that there was no need for additional funding. Rocha and Sternberg (2005) discussed the networking with multinational companies that fostered entrepreneurship in Italy.

According to Peet, "The problem with Italy's small firms is that too many of them are in the wrong industries, relying for too long on cheap labour for their competitive advantage (2005, p. 7)."

9.4 *Toward the Future*

Smiley wrote, "Italy today is richer, better-run and a bit less corrupt than it was ten years ago, but there is still plenty more to do (2001, p. 3)." Kantis (2005) explained how business activities associated with outsourcing the work of other firms were more likely to be taken advantage of in Italy than elsewhere. In Italy, one in three enterprises arose aimed at producing goods previously processed by other companies. This nation has *networks comprised of specialised SMEs*, and already much sub-contracting. For instance, Magatti and Quassoli (forthcoming) explained that unlike the situation in London and New York, the informal SMEs of Milan do not provide low-cost services to people from around the world, working for the world economy. Rather, foreign entrepreneurs in Milan were often providing goods or services to larger firms in the same production sector. Magatti and Quassoli (forthcoming) observed that Italy was increasingly becoming characterised by decentralised and reticular forms of industrial production, including flexible specialisation and industrial districts.

With a sub-contracting market saturated, the future may hold increased success of clusters, as discussed by Pereira and Fernandes (2006). The Italian clusters comprise about 90,000 firms, mostly SMEs. A proof of their efficiency is that they are responsible for around 43% of Italy's exports (Pereira and Fernandes, 2006).

There are three specific types of clusters in Italy: embryonic clusters, consolidated clusters, and mature clusters. As each of these has specific needs, it would be very useful, in the future, to have policies for each of these types. Embryonic clusters would benefit from the reduction of barriers to entry. Consolidated clusters (such as the wooden furniture cluster in Pesaro) have a different set of challenges, as these would benefit from intangible infrastructure for technology transfer. Finally, mature clusters (such as the agro-food cluster in Parma) would benefit from increased internationalisation.[8]

---

[8]For a discussion on the importance of internationalisation of Italian firms, see Pereira *et al.* (2004).

Chapter 10

Luxembourg

10.1 *Introduction*

The Grand Duchy of Luxembourg is a constitutional monarchy (see Exhibit 10.1), covering 2,586 square kilometres, surrounded by Belgium, France and Germany. A founding member of the European Union, Luxembourg is home to the European Court of Auditors, to the European Court of Justice, to the European Investment Bank and to the Secretariat of the European Parliament.

By world standards, Luxembourg is a tiny nation with a disproportionate number of financial institutions. Its importance has exceeded its size, and the nation enjoys the highest per capita GDP in Europe.

Lacking abundance in natural endowment, Luxembourg has created a competitive advantage for itself, by means of innovative policies that facilitate entrepreneurship. Entrepreneurs who cease operations may obtain unemployment benefits when they sign up as job-seekers at an employment agency.

10.2 *Historical Overview*

Luxembourg was part of the Holy Roman Empire, until conquest by France in 1795. In 1815, a grand duchy (see Exhibit 10.2) was created under the House of Orange-Nassau, also rulers of the Netherlands. In 1839, the Walloon-speaking area of Luxembourg was annexed by Belgium. Luxembourg's fortress was one of the few which held back Bismarck during his quest to unify German states.

Exhibit 10.1   At the Palace of the Grand Duke; photo © 2005 Léo-Paul Dana

Until the 1880s, Luxembourg depended on a faltering agrarian economy, but then the duchy welcomed Italians who developed the steel industry.[1] The commercial realm evolved too, and The Companies Law came into effect on August 10, 1915. In 1921, Luxembourg was a founding member of the Benelux customs union. The *Bourse*

---

[1] See Conly (1970).

Exhibit 10.2   Change of the Guard; photo © 2005 Léo-Paul Dana

(Luxembourg Stock Exchange) opened in 1929. During World War II, the Nazis outlawed the French language in Luxembourg (Clark, 1948). Luxembourg was a founding member of the European Coal and Steel Community.

In April 1983, legislation confirmed the legal status of virtually tax-free enterprises in Luxembourg. In 1985, Letzeburgesch became one of the country's three official languages, along with French and German. Following a European Union directive of July 1990, certain small and medium-sized Luxembourg companies became exempt of withholding tax, provided the ownership was within the European Union.

More recently, as the European Union harmonised many policies across its member nations, Luxembourg insisted to maintain its banking secrecy and the absence of withholding taxes on dividends from investments. In January 2003, European Union finance ministers reached an agreement with Luxembourg to impose a withholding tax on bank accounts in Luxembourg, held by non-residents.

10.3   *The Economy, Entrepreneurship & the Small Business Sector*

Luxembourg makes possible the creation of several types of business entities: (i) Société Anonyme (S.A.): an anonymous, incorporated company, common across Europe; (ii) Société à Responsabilité Limité (S.A.R.L.): a firm with limited liability; (iii) 1929-Style Holding Company: a Luxembourg-based S.A. or S.A.R.L. which is largely tax-exempt, according to fiscal legislation passed in July 1929; (iv) Société de Participation Financière (SOPARFI): a holding company, the dividend and capital gains of which can be tax-exempt, according to laws of 1990; and (v) a Luxembourg Trading & Commercial Company: a firm which is not a holding company but which nevertheless has SOPARFI tax-exemptions.

Several factors contribute to an environment conducive to entrepreneurship in Luxembourg (see Exhibit 10.3). Geographically

Exhibit 10.3   View of Pfaffenthal (downtown Luxembourg City) from the *Pont Grande-Duchesse Charlotte*; photo © 2005 Léo-Paul Dana

and politically, the location of Luxembourg within the European Union makes it an ideal hub for distribution. By motorway, Belgium, France and Germany are never more than 26 kilometres from Luxembourg City. The infrastructure is well-developed, with efficient rail links and an international airport six kilometres from Luxembourg City. Luxair is the national flag-carrier.

The financial infrastructure is also very developed. Entrepreneurs in Luxembourg have a wide selection of banks with which to deal. All of the financial institutions are regulated by the Monetary Institute of Luxembourg, locally known by the acronym IML.

Politically, the stability of the duchy is attractive, and the small size of the country helps make public administration easily accessible. From a taxation perspective, Luxembourg is also attractive. When compared to other countries in Europe, the social security contributions are relatively low here. Corporate taxes have a 40% ceiling. In addition to adopting fiscal incentives suggested by the European Union, Luxembourg retained its own. The duchy has over 20 treaties to prevent double taxation. A particular advantage to entrepreneurs based outside Luxembourg is that accounting records need not be kept in the duchy.

Finally, the existence of the 1929-style holding company and of SOPARFI benefits add to the attractiveness of Luxembourg as a centre for entrepreneurship. These firms are allowed a wide range of activities, including access to the *Bourse*. Directors may be of any nationality, and easily-transferred, anonymous shares may be denominated in any currency, in the absence of any exchange control regulations. A 1929-style holding company can be easily converted into a SOPARFI firm, exempted from taxation or capital gains, dividends and liquidation gains.

It is relatively easy to launch a new enterprise in Luxembourg. Shareholders and directors need not be locals. Shares — issued with or without par value — may be either in bearer-form or registered. The presence of over 100 banks makes credit relatively easy to obtain. Listing at the *Bourse* can take as little as 90 days.

Luxembourg is thus an attractive spot from which to launch European operations. Here, the 1929-style holding company may hold cash, negotiables, patents, precious metals and trademarks. It may deposit current assets and finance other firms which are within arm's length. As well, it may borrow capital up to thrice its own issued capital, and it may issue bonds valued up to ten times its equity. It may also buy, hold and sell bonds and shares of other enterprises. Very conveniently, it may receive income from licensing agreements.

By managing a portfolio via such a company, an entrepreneur benefits from legal exemptions; the portfolio incurs neither capital gains tax nor income tax in Luxembourg. The absence of withholding taxes and exchange controls allows the entrepreneur to direct profits to other jurisdictions, as convenient. This has a considerable impact on international networks of entrepreneurs.

10.4   *Toward the Future*

Around the world, governments spend huge sums of money attempting to subsidise entrepreneurship and innovation. How often is this effective? In contrast to those countries that have big budgets to promote entrepreneurship by means of loans and grants, Luxembourg encourages enterprise by means of innovative public policies that are entrepreneurship-friendly and that do not cost much to implement.

Chapter 11

The Netherlands

11.1 *Introduction*

The Netherlands is the European part of the Kingdom of the Netherlands, which since 1954[1] includes the Netherlands Antilles[2] (see Exhibit 11.1). The Netherlands has a surface area of 41,547 square kilometres, including 33,811 square kilometres of land. Its neighbours are Belgium and Germany. The two main western provinces of the Netherlands are Noord (North) Holland and Zuid (South) Holland. With the exception of several pockets such as Volendam,[3] which were traditionally Catholic, the northern part of the Netherlands is generally inhabited by Protestants. The south is largely Catholic.

The Dutch have long been known for their Calvinistic trading spirit, and for the "Dutch engineering genius (Kruisinga, 1933, p. 298)," innovation (Borah, 1938), and technology — including the wind-mills (see Exhibit 11.2) that created polders and expanded available land area (Schot, 1998). McDowell wrote, "People of the Netherlands plug away at problems with characteristic ingenuity (1986, p. 501)." Ulijn *et al.* (2001) found that although Dutch and Germans engineers

---

[1]In 1986, the Caribbean island of Aruba was separated from the Netherlands Antilles and became an autonomous part of the kingdom.

[2]For a discussion of entrepreneurship in the Netherlands Antilles, see Dana (1990).

[3]Volendam was formerly a fishing port on the salt water Zuiderzee, opening to the North Sea; the Zuiderzee was dammed in 1932, forming an inland, freshwater lake, Ijssel Meer. For contemporary accounts and details of the Zuiderzee project, see Kruisinga (1933) and Mumford (1938).

Exhibit 11.1   Curacao; photo © 2005 Léo-Paul Dana

Exhibit 11.2   Windmills; photo © 2005 Léo-Paul Dana

have a common professional culture, the transition from technological orientation to market orientation occurred earlier among Dutch engineers. In another comparison, Ulijn and Fayolle suggested, "The Dutch government does not mingle too much with the national economy affairs... whereas the French and the German governments do a lot more and protect their much bigger domestic markets (2004, p. 211)." Comparing France and the Netherlands, Ulijn and Fayolle wrote, "The Netherlands seems to have a stronger entrepreneurial culture... The Dutch are more impressed with actions than words (2004, p. 216)."

Exhibit 11.3   Fokker Tri-motor; photo © 2005 Léo-Paul Dana

Exhibit 11.4   Fokker F-7 of Pan American; photo courtesy of Pan Am

Famous Dutch entrepreneurs include aircraft manufacturer Anton Herman Gerard "Anthony" Fokker[4] (see Exhibit 11.3 and Exhibit 11.4) born in the Dutch East Indies, Albert Plesman, founder of KLM Royal Dutch Airlines, and beer leader Alfred H. "Freddy" Heineken. Philips, Shell, and Unilever also began here.

---

[4] See Ulijn and Heerkens (1999).

11.2 *Historical Overview*

The Netherlands were once a part of the Roman Empire, and later a part of Charlemagne's empire. During the 15th century, the Dutch were ruled by dukes of Burgundy. In 1555, these lands came under Spanish rule, and Dutch Protestants were poorly treated by Spaniards.

William of Orange, German Count of Nassau, inherited vast possessions in the Netherlands, and initiated the struggle for independence from Spain, and ultimately the creation of the republic of the United Netherlands, which became known for its religious tolerance. In 1568, the Low Countries demanded autonomy and religious freedom from Spain. Villiers noted, "As early as 1579, a treaty that united the seven northern provinces guaranteed freedom of religion (1968, p. 532)."

McDowell wrote about this country, "Historically, the Netherlands has always been a haven for refugees: Jews fleeing the Iberian Inquisitions, Huguenots forced out of France, even English Pilgrims... (1986, p. 502)." As explained by Rath, "In the sixteenth and seventeenth centuries large groups of Protestants from southern Netherlands and France migrated to Amsterdam... These immigrants possessed plenty of capital, trading contacts and skills (2002, p. 149)."

"From the end of the sixteenth century on, large groups of Portuguese (Sephardic) Jews arrived in Mokum[5]... also Ashkenazic Jews from Central and East Europe. These immigrants became involved with trade and industry, partly due to the fact that they were excluded from various occupations by the non-Jewish majority (Rath, 2002, p. 149)." Excluded from traditional guilds, during the late 16th century, Jews established a diamond cutting industry in Amsterdam.[6]

Rath and Kloosterman noted, "The arrival of Jews from the Iberian Peninsula in the sixteenth century and later from Eastern Europe, and of

---

[5]Nickname for Amsterdam.
[6]For a detailed account of Amsterdam, see Davenport (1974).

Exhibit 11.5   Portuguese *Esnoga*; photo © 2005 Léo-Paul Dana

Roman Catholics from Westphalia throughout the nineteenth century, greatly influenced the Dutch economic landscape as their business acumen enhanced the nation's economic and cultural wealth (2003, pp. 123–124)." Speaking of the Dutch, Sombart wrote "they were fully alive to the gain which the Jews brought (1913, p. 19)." Exhibit 11.5 shows the Portuguese synagogue built in Amsterdam during the 17th century.

The 17th century became known as the golden age of the Netherlands, as the Dutch Republic became a leading commercial power, with its innovative *Verenigde Oostindische Compagnie* (United East India Company) playing an important role in the Indonesian archipelago.[7] This was one of several companies established in European countries to conduct trade with the Orient. The Dutch East India Company was established in 1602 and traded largely in spices. The Dutch

---

[7] For a history of entrepreneurship in Indonesia, see Dana (1999c).

West India Company was created by Dutch entrepreneurs in 1621, for the purpose of conducting trade with Africa and the Americas; on the island of Manhattan, this firm built Fort Amsterdam — which later became New York City. The Dutch West India Company continued trading until 1674.

In 1795, France invaded the Netherlands and the Dutch East India Company was liquidated the following year. France continued to occupy the Netherlands and in 1806 Napoleon made it a kingdom for his brother Louis. In 1813, the Dutch and Belgian provinces were united into the Netherlands. In 1815, Willem became King of the Netherlands. In 1830, Belgium became its own country.

In Amsterdam, during the 19th century, Westphalian Catholics and East European Jews gravitated to the *schmata* (textiles and clothing) business (Raes, 2000). "In the second half of the nineteenth century, Roman Catholic immigrants of Westphalian origin settled in the city (Rath, 2002, p. 149)."

Emma was the regent of the Netherlands from 1890 to 1898, when her daughter Queen Wilhemina[8] ascended to the throne at the age of 18. Modernisation and industrialisation took place during the late 19th century.[9] The early 20th century in the Netherlands is well documented by Rice (1925). Kerbey (1940) observed that Rotterdam[10] grew to be Europe's largest port, until its invasion by the Nazis in 1940.[11] Thanks to laborious efforts during the post-war years,[12] Rotterdam soon regained its rank as the world's busiest port.[13]

---

[8] Queen Wilhemina eventually abdicated in favour of her daughter Juliana Louise Emma Marie Wilhemina.

[9] See respectively: Grin *et al.* (2004) and Kooij (1997).

[10] For accounts of Rotterdam's shipping role, see Kerbey (1940) and Miller (1960).

[11] For an account of the World War II experience, see Henry (1946).

[12] For discussions of the post-war years in the Netherlands, see Clark (1950) and Grosvenor and Neave (1954).

[13] See Graves (1967).

Rath and Kloosterman noted changing demographics, "In the wake of the Second World War, and after the decolonisation in Indonesia, a group of Moluccans arrived in 1951 as did cohorts of people of Dutch or Dutch-Asian origin (2003, p. 125)." Also during the 1950s, many Dutch people emigrated from the Netherlands and established themselves (often as entrepreneurs), in Canada, New Zealand and beyond. In 1959, a close alliance between Belgium, Luxembourg and the Netherlands resulted in the Benelux economic union.

When Israel was invaded in October 1973, the Netherlands took a pro-Israel stance (Davenport, 1974). Following the oil embargo, the Dutch government implemented a ban on Sunday driving. In 1975, Suriname gained its independence.

During the 1970s, the Netherlands continued to welcome immigrants, many of whom created new ventures, "to supply the specific needs of newcomers for food, clothing, and entertainment (Boissevain and Grotenbreg 1989, p. 223)." In general, however, "small firms were believed to be doomed. The prevalent economic theories of left-wing and mainstream economists alike predicted that only large firms would be able to survive in a modern capitalist economy (Rath and Kloosterman, 2003, p. 125)."

In 1980, Queen Juliana Louise Emma Marie Wilhemina abdicated in favour of her daughter Beatrix[14] Wilhemina Armgard. In 1984, the Dutch government launched an Innovation Stimulation Scheme to subsidise small and medium-sized information technology firms. In 1986, the World Economic Forum identified the Netherlands as the most internationally-oriented among 21 Western economies.

By 1987, "more than 7,000 of the 350,000 registered small and medium-sized businesses[15] in the Netherlands (Boissevain and

---

[14] Queen Beatrix is from the House of Orange-Nassau, rulers of the Netherlands since 1814.

[15] Boissevain and Grotenbreg explained, "In the Netherlands, enterprises employing up to 99 employees are considered small or medium-sized (1987, p. 128)."

Grotenbreg, 1987, p. 105)" were ethnic enterprises. Yet, Boissevain and Grotenbreg (1987) noted that self-employment was much *less* common among immigrant groups in the Netherlands, than in mainstream Dutch society.

Boissevain and Grotenbreg (1988) focused on the many immigrants from Suriname who became self-employed in Amsterdam. The authors observed that Hindustani immigrants from Suriname were more parsimonious than Creoles from Suriname, and that the Hindustanis were overwhelmingly active as shopkeepers whereas Creoles from Suriname chiefly owned restaurants and cafés.

Amsterdam (see Exhibit 11. 6) was a contender to host the 1992 Olympic Games. In 1997, "the Dutch government launched an initiative aimed at supporting start-up firms... (Nijkamp *et al.*, 2004, p. 44)." Today, Amsterdam is an important hub for transportation (see Exhibit 11.7) and telecommunications (see Exhibit 11.8).

Exhibit 11.6   Amsterdam; photo © 2005 Léo-Paul Dana

Exhibit 11.7 Central Station in Amsterdam; photo © 2005 Léo-Paul Dana

Exhibit 11.8 The Dutch Postal System is among the Best in the World; photo © 2005 Léo-Paul Dana

11.3   *The Economy, Entrepreneurship & the Small Business Sector*

New ventures in the Netherlands have been regulated since the Depression. "In 1935, conditions for establishing an enterprise in Amsterdam were formulated for the first time… In 1937 the Establishment of Small Business Act came into effect at the national level… The object of this act and the 1954 Business Establishment Act was to promote orderly entrepreneurial activity (Boissevain and Grotenbreg, 1989, p. 230)."

Until the 1980s, "people who wanted to start a business were legally required to have appropriate qualifications and permits to register (Rath, 2003, p. 277)." Then came a period of deregulation, and eventually support for entrepreneurs. Dana *et al.* argued that "generous support for small and medium-sized companies through a network of 18 Innovation Centers attest to a deliberate national policy for promoting the growth of new enterprises. Indeed, many people think that recent economic reforms in the Netherlands offer a successful half-way house between Anglo-American free markets and continental European welfare states. It has even been given a name: the *polder-model* (2000, p. 192)." The polder-model involves policymaking by consensus[16] among the state, employers and unions (see Peet, 2002).

Villiers wrote about the Dutch, "A nation of individualists? Yes, perhaps — but when necessary, surely the most cooperative individualists in the world (1968, p. 571)." Likewise, the *Netherlands Report on Competition Law and Institutions*, OECD Document DAF/COM D, published in 2005, referred to the Netherlands as a country with a tradition of co-operation.

Dutch entrepreneurs can be excellent team players, as evident from their successful clusters. Among these is the flower industry; Dutch flowers represent 65% of the worldwide exports of cut flowers. Dutch flower

---

[16]For a discussion of consensus in Dutch firms, see d'Iribane (1989).

producers have innovated at all levels of the value chain, increasing productivity, reducing production costs, improving quality and increasing competitiveness (Pereira and Fernandes, 2006).

Boissevain and Grotenbreg (1987) suggested that *access to a network of contacts is an entrepreneurial resource* in the Netherlands. The authors noted that networks can provide introductions to wholesalers and warning of government inspection, among other things.

Kloosterman *et al.* (1998) showed that immigrants to the Netherlands are heavily involved in informal methods of production. They argued that on the demand side, "the scope for informal activities has increased because of trends towards disintegration of activities in manufacturing and especially in service industries, the fragmentation of consumer markets, a gradual emergence of a demand for 'ethnic' products, and also owing to the dynamics of so called 'vacancy chains' (1998, p. 249)." The authors explained that immigrants "usually set up their businesses in those sectors where informal production could give them a competitive edge. Through their networks of relatives, co-nationals or co-ethnics they have privileged and flexible access to information, capital and — with relatively low monetary costs — labour (1998, p. 249)."

Rath and Kloosterman (2003) observed that entrepreneurs from China, Suriname, Turkey, India, and Pakistan in Amsterdam create economies of scope, "Immigrants have been especially active in the food sector... The *raison d'être* of their businesses originates in part from their capacity to create economies of scope. They sometimes specialise in specific ranges of products, including 'ethnic' or religious products such as kosher or halal food[17] (Rath and Kloosterman, 2003, p. 123)."

During the late 20th century, a crisis facing Philips and DAF Trucks[18] resulted in the creation of 300 new technology-based firms

---

[17] For an explanation, see Kloosterman *et al.* (1998).
[18] DAF Trucks merged with British Leyland.

in the Eindhoven area (Noord Brabant province), in the southeast of the Netherlands.

The Global Entrepreneurship Monitor (GEM) reports suggest that early-stage entrepreneurial activity has been on the decline, and structural factors have been identified among the causal variables. The Dutch entrepreneurial climate is discussed in detail in the 2001 GEM study by Bosma *et al.* (2002). It appears that potential entrepreneurs are discouraged by negative risk attitudes and by employment conditions and social security, resulting in high opportunity costs in the Netherlands.

The 2003 GEM study reveals that the Total Entrepreneurial Activity Index of the Netherlands is relatively low when compared to Belgium, Sweden, Germany, Denmark, the United Kingdom, Spain, Greece, Finland, Ireland and other countries. In their 2005 *Index of Economic Freedom*, Miles *et al.* (2005) showed that there is a very high fiscal burden of government in the Netherlands.

11.4   *Toward the Future*

In contrast to the many places where culture does not accept entrepreneurship as socially desirable activity, Dutch culture views entrepreneurship favourably (see Exhibit 11.9). Many Dutch people say that they are qualified for entrepreneurship, and they see opportunities. Yet, few choose to pursue an entrepreneurship career. The majority appear to be risk averse.

Social norms in the Netherlands are positive with respect to esteem for entrepreneurs. Earlier barriers to entrepreneurship, including regulation, have been reduced. The formal venture capital market is well developed. Access to physical infrastructure is also good. Other factors, however, decrease the attractiveness of the entrepreneurship sector. Education, for instance, does little to contribute to entrepreneurship. Furthermore, social security and the welfare system do not encourage

Exhibit 11.9   Fond of Entrepreneurs; photo © 2005 Léo-Paul Dana

people to take initiative. Perhaps they should, in particular in the case of relating entrepreneurship to innovation.

Ulijn and Fayolle summarised the situation by stating that "starting your own business is perceived as rather difficult, but in the Netherlands less so than in the EU in general (2004, p. 211)." They noted that "the Dutch are per capita (77) more productive than the EU average (65)… but the Dutch managerial culture seems to lead to a lot less willingness to start your own business (41%) than the U.S. (2004, pp. 211–214)."

Chapter 12

Portugal

12.1 *Introduction*

Portugal shares the Iberian Peninsula with Spain, and extends to neighbouring islands, covering 91,905 square kilometres. It was the "earliest and once the greatest of Europe's modern imperial powers (La Fay, 1965, p. 453)." Portugal ruled over Brazil (see Exhibit 12.1), Angola (see Exhibit 12.2), Mozambique (see Exhibit 12.3), Macao (see Exhibit 12.4) and beyond. Portugal's wines (see Exhibit 12.5) were exported around the world.

After the independence of the Portuguese colonies, which took place following the revolution of April, 25, 1974 (also referred to as the Cravos[1] Revolution), the political and social conditions in the former colonies became problematic. This prompted the exodus of Europeans, who lived in the colonies, to move to the Portuguese mainland. This, in turn, resulted in a huge increase in people seeking employment in Portugal, while jobs became relatively scarce. As a result, many of the so-called *retornados* (returned people, from the colonies) became self-employed.

In most of Europe, the most common source of capital for new ventures is the entrepreneur himself; in Portugal, financial institutions are the principle source of funds. Yet, Portuguese people who find work tend to prefer the security of employment, over the risks inherent in

---

[1] *Cravos* is the name of a flower that people wore during that revolution to symbolise freedom.

166

Exhibit 12.1   Portuguese Architecture in Brazil; photo © 2005 Léo-Paul Dana

Exhibit 12.2   Angola; photo © 2005 Léo-Paul Dana

entrepreneurship. The general mindset, in Portugal, reflects an attitude of risk aversion, and the dominance of existing firms contributes to the barriers to entry. Although entrepreneurship is socially acceptable in Portugal, it is not an enticing career path for most Portuguese. Silva and Hall noted, "Portugal is a country where inequalities of power and wealth may hinder the scope for opportunity… it is further characterised

Exhibit 12.3   Lourenço Marques Was the Capital of Portuguese Mozambique; photo © 2005 Léo-Paul Dana

Exhibit 12.4   Macao; photo © 2005 Léo-Paul Dana

Exhibit 12.5   Quality Vines; photo © 2005 Léo-Paul Dana

by low tolerance of uncertainty and it is, consequently, a rule oriented country where bureaucracy and controls are very much instituted, a situation in clear contrast with the easiness to accept change and the readiness to take risks… (2005, pp. 331–332)."

12.2 *Historical Overview*

Except for a brief period of Spanish rule, Portugal has been independent since the 12th century. During the 16th century, "Portugal changed the map of the world by her epochal achievements in discovery (Moore, 1938, p. 133)." In 1506, Portugal began ruling Mozambique as part of Portuguese India.

In 1553, officials in Guangdong accepted bribes from the Portuguese who wished to conduct trade in Macao. The Japanese were willing to buy Chinese silk, but the Celestial Empire prohibited business dealings between Chinese and Japanese merchants; when Portuguese entrepreneurs discovered this, they prospered as middlemen[2] between the two Asian powers.

In 1557, China allowed Portuguese merchants to establish homes and warehouses in Macao. The Portuguese supplied ivory from Africa and cotton from Goa, as well as cannons, clocks and mirrors from Europe. In exchange, Chinese entrepreneurs brought porcelain, seed pearls and silk. Exporting silk from Macao to Japan proved to be highly profitable for the Portuguese entrepreneurs who were happy to be paid in silver. They then used the silver to pay for Chinese goods, which they sold in Europe.

In 1887, Portugal forced China to sign the Draft Agreement of the Sino-Portuguese Meeting. This was followed by the Sino-Portuguese Treaty of Peking, allowing Portugal perpetual administration of Macao.[3] In Mozambique (see Exhibit 12.6), the slave trade flourished until the 20th century.

In Portugal, however, there was poverty (see Exhibit 12.7) and social discontentment, and this led to the Portuguese monarch being deposed in 1910. On October 5, of the same year, Portugal was proclaimed the Portuguese Republic.

The creation of a republic was symbolic of the hope for progress, freedom and social justice. A problem arose when the new regime was incapable of changing the fragile economic, social and political situation with which Portugal was struggling. As a result, instability and population discontentment escalated.

Social institutions lost importance. The state faced budgeting crises, as there was a continuous deficit in the commercial balance. The state sold gold to provide for external expenses. Inflation escalated, and

---

[2] For discussions of entrepreneurship in middleman minorities, see Auster and Aldrich (1984); Bonacich (1973); Cherry (1990); Dana (1997); and Loewen (1971).

[3] Macao was an Overseas Province of Portugal from 1961 until 1974. In April 1987, Portugal signed the Joint Sino-Portuguese Declaration and Basic Law, allowing the PRC to take back Macao, on December 20, 1999.

Exhibit 12.6   Municipal Market in Maputo (formerly Lourenço Marques); photo © 2005 Léo-Paul Dana

the currency lost its value. Public goods were sold at less than market value. All of these were conducive to the Military Action on May 28 1926, out of which the New State was created.

Between 1926 and 1945, tight political control measures clearly threatened any entrepreneurial initiative. Measures included: (i) the Colonial Act of 1930; (ii) the Wheat Campaign of 1930–1940; (iii) the Law of Industrial Conditioning, in 1931; (iv) the Law of Economic

Exhibit 12.7   Rural Portugal; photo © 2005 Léo-Paul Dana

Restructure, in 1935; (v) the Law of Internal Colonisation, in 1937; (vi) the Law of Hydro-agricultural Promotion, and the Law of Forest Populating, in 1938; (vii) the Law of National Electricity, in 1944; and (viii) the Law of the Industrial Promotion and Reorganisation, in 1945. These, coupled with the Law of Import Substitution, created significant restrictions, and most trade was conducted with the colonies. Portugal agreed with its colonies that they would supply the raw materials Portugal would need and in exchange they would receive manufactured products from the mainland. As a result, there was an intensification of the production of primary products, such as cotton, in all the colonies.

In 1951, Angola and Mozambique became overseas provinces of Portugal. In 1953, the Portuguese ordered indigenous Mozambicans to leave their farms and villages to clear more land for forced cotton growing (see Exhibit 12.8). Under the supervision of ruthless overseers, each family was also obliged to grow cassava (see Exhibit 12.9) and

Exhibit 12.8 The Train Station in the National Capital Was the Transportation Hub; photo © 2005 Léo-Paul Dana

sorghum. Immigrants from Asia, however, were exempt from forced labour, and were allowed to operate their private small businesses.

According to the 1955 census, 65% of the Europeans in Mozambique were still illiterate at the time. Illiteracy among indigenous Africans in Mozambique was even higher. In 1962, an independent movement was established. It came to be known as the *Frente de Liberação de Moçambique* (Front for the Liberation of Mozambique), also referred to as Frelimo. It initiated a violent revolution in 1964.

The issue of political, economic and social instability extended to all Portuguese provinces, leading to colonial war. As such, the 1960s was an eventful decade for Portugal, experiencing the colonial war, and also the movement towards the European integration, the internationalisation of the economy and emigration.

Four decades of conservative dictatorship ended in a *coup d'état,* in April 1974. In June, the republic announced that it was giving independence to Angola and to Mozambique. As a result, at least

Exhibit 12.9   Cassava; photo © 2005 Léo-Paul Dana

180,000 Europeans in Africa moved to Portugal. Graves reported, "Today thousands of small businesses and professional jobs are filled by retornados (1980, p. 815)." While the United Kingdom gave Hong Kongers a British National Overseas Passport, which does not entitle the bearer to reside in Britain, Portugal gave Portuguese citizenship to the Macanese.

Economic development escalated in 1986, when Portugal joined the European Community. In 1988, the Reform of the Community Structural Funds largely benefited Portugal through the deployment of the Support Community Frames. Operational programmes were defined mostly with structural goals. Then came major investments in infrastructure, and in the education of the Portuguese (including the working population, the students, the long-term unemployed and the handicapped). Simultaneously, programmes emerged aimed at supporting entrepreneurial initiative and with them the creation of supporting institutions to both the incumbents and the new companies. In 1989, Portugal embarked on a large scale privatisation programme. The Portuguese currency became fully convertible in 1992.

In July 2002, Portugal launched the Programme for Productivity and Economic Growth, with an axis addressed to supporting innovation, research and development. A concern in 2003 was that inflation in Portugal clearly exceeded the European Union average (Simões, 2004).

12.3   *The Economy, Entrepreneurship & the Small Business Sector*

Traditionally, fishing was of great importance to Portugal. Conger (1948) wrote about thousands of self-employed fish peddlers, women known as fishwives. A few years later, Villiers reported, "In Portugal, fishermen are formed into 'companies' perhaps 80 men strong, and the 'companions' (as the members of a company are called) have the right by ancient custom to fish enough to keep their families going and get a share of all profits on the catch. If there are no profits, they still eat (1954, p. 680)." Pickerell (1968) wrote about fishing during the 1960s. Many Portuguese relied on the primary sector (see Exhibit 12.10) for subsistence.

Since the Portuguese economy had hermetically closed itself to the outside, entrepreneurial spirit was obliterated outside subsistence self-employment (see Exhibit 12.11). History changed paths in 1976, as Portugal began to prepare itself to join the European Economic Community a decade later.

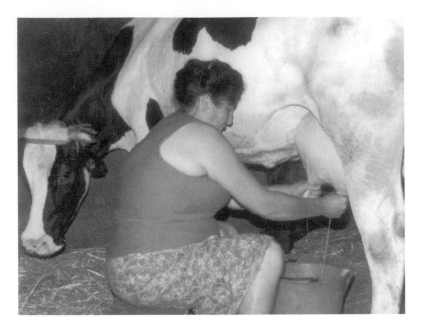

Exhibit 12.10   Milk for the Day; photo © 2005 Léo-Paul Dana

Exhibit 12.11   Self-employed; photo © 2005 Léo-Paul Dana

The 2001 *Global Entrepreneurship Monitor Portugal Report* (GEM), by the Faculty of Economics at the *Universidade Nova Economia*, was one of the first systematic, large-scale studies of entrepreneurship in Portugal; the study revealed a significant lack of entrepreneurial activity in this country. Follow-up studies were not conducted in 2002 or 2003, and at the time of writing, in 2005, the 2001 report was the only one available for Portugal. Among the sponsors of the Portugal GEM was the *Instituto de Apoio às Pequenas e Médias Empresas e ao Investimento* that operates under the supervision of the Ministry of Economy; this institute conceives policies, and implements initiatives in the attempts to make Portuguese players more competitive, thus contributing to the achievement of the nation's economic goals.

Portugal was found to have relatively open markets and a good infrastructure facilitating entrepreneurship. Unlike the case in many other countries, Portugal offers tax benefits with regards to R&D expenditures, as these are considered current costs. The GEM report found that Portugal ranked better than Germany or Belgium, but worse than France or Ireland, in terms of total entrepreneurial activity.

The GEM study found that respondents perceived more entrepreneurship opportunities in Portugal than was the case elsewhere, but acted less on these opportunities; the report suggested that this could be evidence of barriers to entrepreneurial activity in Portugal. There appears to be powerful barriers to entry, including inflexible employment regulations that put undue strain on entrepreneurs.

Constraints include imbalance in governmental programme planning; the lack of effective entrepreneurship training; and underdevelopment in support services. It appears that training programmes sometimes do not correspond to actual needs.

A further constraint appears to be difficulty in accessing finance, largely due to lack of awareness of existing sources of capital. According to the European Venture Capital Association, the amount of venture capital investment in the early stages is near the average for countries

when compared to other countries. This usually has a negative impact on national competitiveness.

On the positive side, opportunities include: the introduction of new technologies to revitalise traditional sectors; the further development of existing clusters; and internationalisation by means of symbiotic networking.[4]

---

[4] See Dana *et al.* (forthcoming).

Chapter 13

Spain

13.1 Introduction

Spain covers 504,782 square kilometres on the Iberian Peninsula, the Balearic Islands in the Mediterranean and the Canary Islands[1] in the Atlantic Ocean. Spain's neighbours are Portugal to the west, the Rock of Gibraltar[2] (see Exhibit 13.1) to the south and Andorra and France to the north. The Basques[3] constitute an important minority in Spain; entrepreneurship has traditionally been high[4] among this distinct group. The comparative study of entrepreneurial frameworks reveals that the Basque Country ranks higher than other regions, in key issues such as government programmes for entrepreneurship — including financial support.

The Global Entrepreneurship Monitor (GEM) has already had a positive impact in Spain, promoting the reduction of administrative burdens for entrepreneurs, entrepreneurial attitudes in the educational system, a focus on financing and the fostering of entrepreneurship.

Among Spain's leading entrepreneurs is fashion-king Amancio Ortega Gaona. Spain's richest man, he is the founder of the Inditex Group, which has more than 14,000 employees. His retail shops are called Zara.

---

[1] Shor and Shor (1955) focus on the Canary Islands.
[2] For a discussion of entrepreneurship in Gibraltar, see Dana (2002).
[3] For discussions of the Basque people and their land, see Nolan (1954) and Abercrombie (1995).
[4] For a discussion of entrepreneurship among the Basques in Spain, see Dana (1995b); for a discussion of Basque entrepreneurs in the United States, see Laxalt (1966).

Exhibit 13.1   Gibraltar; photo © 2005 Léo-Paul Dana

13.2 *Historical Overview*

Formerly ruled as separate kingdoms,[5] Spain was united in 1492, through the marriage of Ferdinand II of Aragon and Isabella of Castile. Later that year, the Moors lost Grenada. Soon, Spain became the most powerful country of Europe, controlling much of the Americas (see Exhibit 13.2). In time, the colonies achieved independence. In 1929, the Ibero-American Exposition served as a reunion between Spain and her former colonies.[6]

Just prior[7] to the Spanish Civil War, Kihn wrote, "Next to agriculture, mining is Spain's most important source of wealth (1936, p. 410)." The war[8] lasted from July 1936 to March 1939, when a new regime was led by General Francisco Franco. He banned the use of the Basque, Catalan and Galician languages in public. During the 1950s, rural Spain experienced a flight from poverty to Madrid.[9]

In the words of Bryson, "Until well into the 1960s Spain was one of the poorest countries in Western Europe (1992, p. 8)." By the middle of

---

[5]There were three Christian kingdoms in the north (Asturias, Catalonia and Navarre), while the south had Moorish rulers.

[6]For a detailed discussion of Spain's Ibero-American Exposition, see Ford (1929).

[7]For an account of Spain before the war, see Adams (1929), and McBride (1929; 1931).

[8]For a war-time account of the Spanish Civil War, see McBride (1936).

[9]For an account of urbanisation in Spain, see Putman (1986).

Exhibit 13.2   La Serena (Chile), Established 1544; photo © 2005 Léo-Paul Dana

the decade, however, McDowell noted, "Many economists predict that Spain is beginning an economic take-off similar to Italy's after World War II (1965, p. 297)." This had a positive impact on some people, but not on others. Laxalt reported a Spanish interviewee as saying, "I lost my two sons to progress… Times are changing… But I don't know why they should (1974, p. 796)." In 1974, the *Instituto de Estudios Superiores de la Empresa* introduced a course in entrepreneurship (Dana, 1992b).

Franco died in 1975, and Juan Carlos became King of Spain. The Basque, Catalan and Galician languages reappeared. In 1978, in response to demands for increased local autonomy, the constitution decentralised power. In 1980, three Spanish provinces, namely Álava,

Guipúzcoa, and Vizcaya were united to form the Basques Autonomous Community; these were traditionally the industrial vanguard of the Iberian Peninsula. Regional differences remained, and in their study, Galicia *et al.* found that "industrialisation in previously rural areas is not an automatic panacea for problems generated by unequal distribution of wealth (1992, p. 102)."

In 1986, Spain joined the European Economic Community, undertook a privatisation programme and began liberalising the economy. Infrastructure was improved (see Exhibit 13.3). Telecommunications (see Exhibit 13.4) were modernised (see Exhibit 13.5). Ports were upgraded (see Exhibit 13.6). Firms became increasingly market-oriented (see Exhibit 13.7). Planning began (see Exhibit 13.8) for the 1992 World's Fair, Expo '92 (see Exhibit 13.9). By the early 1990s, Bryson (1992) noted that Spanish society was becoming increasingly secular. Seville (which had held the 1929 World's Fair) hosted millions

Exhibit 13.3   Upgrading the Infrastructure; photo © 2005 Léo-Paul Dana

Exhibit 13.4   Classic Mail Box; photo © 2005 Léo-Paul Dana

of visitors at Expo '92, which opened in April 1992 (see Exhibit 13.10). The pavilion of Spain is featured in Exhibit 13.11.

In 1993, the Basque government set to zero the corporation tax for newly established entrepreneurs. The central government of Spain decided to challenge this move on the premise that it would prejudice neighbouring regions where entrepreneurship is less prevalent and the environment is less conducive to entrepreneurial activity. Red tape was already lean in the Basque country, while work ethic, entrepreneurial culture and government incentives were keeping Basques at the forefront of economic development. Also in 1993, research found that two-way sub-contracting among Madrid's electronics producers was already

Exhibit 13.5   Modern Look; photo © 2005 Léo-Paul Dana

substantially higher than among similar firms in Austria and Sweden (Suárez-Villa and Rama, 1996).

Spain has been a regular participant of the GEM study since 2000. The GEM team consists of Alicia Coduras, Ignacio de la Vega, Rachida Justo, and Cristina Cruz, based at the Empresa Business School, in Madrid (see Exhibit 13.12).

Exhibit 13.6   Improved Facilities; photo © 2005 Léo-Paul Dana

Exhibit 13.7   Iberia Advertising in Tangiers (طنجة); photo © 2005 Léo-Paul Dana

Exhibit 13.8   Preparing for the Fair; photo © 2005 Léo-Paul Dana

13.3   *The Economy, Entrepreneurship & the Small Business Sector*

Shortly after the turn of the century, Van Auken and de Lema observed:

> Economic growth in Spain has primarily been based on the increase of productivity that resulted from intensive capital investment and technical growth... SMEs have had an important role in Spanish economic growth. During 1996–2000, for example, the number of new firms increased by more than 200,000 firms. The predominance of SMEs in the Spanish economy is evident from the large proportion of the micro-firms relative to other European countries (2003, p. 19).

SMEs in Spain often work together, and are heavily involved in sub-contracting, sometimes in geographic clusters.[10] Rama *et al.* (2003)

---

[10] See also Padmore and Gibson (1997).

Exhibit 13.9   Completed on Time; photo © 2005 Léo-Paul Dana

noted that over 84% of Spanish electronics production is concentrated in Madrid, Catalonia and the Basque Country. They elaborated, "While Catalonia specialises in consumer electronics (82% of Spanish production) and the Basque Country in industrial electronics (70%), Madrid is Spain's most important producer of telecommunications equipment (77%) and defence and industrial electronics (59%)… (Rama *et al.*, 2003, p. 76)." As explained by Suárez-Villa and Rama (1996), *Madrid's electronics sector is a complex web of interdependent firms.*

Exhibit 13.10   The Monorail; photo © 2005 Léo-Paul Dana

Exhibit 13.11   The Pavilion of Spain; photo © 2005 Léo-Paul Dana

Exhibit 13.12   Madrid; photo © 2005 Léo-Paul Dana

In contrast, Catalonia has a hub-and-spoke structure, with multinationals ringed by Spanish sub-contractors. The relationship among firms is symbiotic.

Rama *et al.* noted that "the small electronics plants located in the Basque Country tend to supply other regional industries, such as machine tools, as specialised, or possibly strategic subcontractors… Linkages between electronics firms are highly concentrated in Madrid and the Basque Country… In Catalonia, by contrast, the coordination between consumer electronics multinationals and their subcontractors is less intensive (2003, p. 76)." Rama *et al.* added, "While Madrid lacks many of the common socio-cultural values that define classical industrial districts, it is home to a vibrant community of engineering professionals and supporting occupational institutions (2003, p. 77)." Thus, most sub-contracting in Madrid's electronics sector can (and does) take place within the Madrid region (Rama and Calatrava, 2002). Rama *et al.* further explained, "Madrid's sampled electronics producers seem to seek complementaries with other companies, not just the flexibility of enlarging their working force during short periods of work overload. This contrasts with the hub-and-spoke district, which relies more on networks of capacity subcontractors. The motivation of externalising production is not significantly associated with establishment or firm size, suggesting that both small and large producers alike participate in a network characterised by specialised, or collaborative subcontracting (2003, p. 83)."

The GEM report (Coduras *et al.*, 2005) revealed that 39% of the Spanish active population perceived the existence of good opportunities in 2004, up from 2003. This indicates an improvement in the climate for the business creation. Yet, the Total Entrepreneurial Activity Index (TEA) for 2004 was 5.15, down by 23.93% since 2003. This reflects a recession,[11] although not of great magnitude. Nevertheless, the TEA for 2004 was above the average for European Union member states and very similar to the TEA indexes of Denmark and the Netherlands. The data for 2004 showed that the percentage of businesses that did not have any expectation of expansion fell by 28.2%, suggesting increased hope for growth.

In 2004, men were still more than twice as likely to be involved in entrepreneurship as women in Spain and the actual rate of female involvement fell 8.3% with respect to 2003. Informal investment activity in Spain decreased 24.7% in 2004 with respect to 2003.

Of the eight Spanish regions analysed by the GEM team in 2004 (Andalucía, the Basque Country, Castilla León, the Canaries, Cataluña, Extremadura, Madrid and Valencia), the least active in terms of

---

[11]The recessive economic climate was perhaps partly brought about by the political turmoil that resulted after terrorist attacks in Madrid in March.

entrepreneurship was the region of the Canary Islands. Extremadura — historically the least developed region in Spain — was found to be the most enterprising in 2004. Its Total Entrepreneurship Activity index, with two percentage points above the Spanish average, indicates that the region is gradually catching up with the rest of Spain.

In his comparative study of entrepreneurs in Italy and in Spain, Kantis (2005) found that networks of Spanish entrepreneurs reflect the greater relative importance of their relatives and friends, whereas in Italy, business relations are more common. He found that Spanish business networks are relatively unstable when compared to those in Italy, suggesting that connections are weaker. Among his respondents, those in Spain emphasised to a greater degree than did those in Italy, the influence of the family in shaping attitudes and creating a work ethic.

13.4   *Toward the Future*

De Clercq *et al.* wrote, "Ireland, Spain and Finland score highest for opportunity entrepreneurship (2004, p. 19)." However, Spain is facing worrying trends. Of the nine key areas that have a direct effect on entrepreneurial activity, there is a general negative trend in financial support, education and training, research and development and market openness. Other important factors are experiencing slow improvements, such as the country's post-secondary educational system, governmental policies for entrepreneurship and cultural and social norms. The latter, experts say, is fostered by the openness of Spain to the Western world, which is inducing a gradual change in mentality and an increasing social acceptance of entrepreneurs. Among the areas perceived as needing improvement, experts recommend the creation of financial support mechanisms that are tailored to SMEs, a diffusion of information regarding existent government programmes and the establishment of new ones targeting specially disadvantaged groups such as women and

Exhibit 13.13   Thinking Back at the Good Old Days; photo © 2005 Léo-Paul Dana

persons older than 50 years of age (see Exhibit 13.13). In a country with a long tradition of civil servants, efforts should also be focused on creating a framework to develop an entrepreneurial spirit, as early as childhood.

Chapter 14

Symbiotic Entrepreneurship in the Euro-zone

14.1 *A Heterogeneous Euro-zone*

Chan and Justis (1992) correctly predicted the importance of cultural differences in Europe, well after economic integration; they emphasised local preferences over a "pan-European (1992, p. 85)" ideal. As stated by Kaynak and Jallat, "Throughout history, Europe has been able to retain its multitude of cultures, varied social organisations, distinct forms of expression, and disparate modes of thought (2004, p. 4)." Even today, Europe is not a mass market, "but a culturally and linguistically diverse market with a number of divergent markets (Kaynak and Jallat, 2004, p. 6)." The preceding chapters confirm that entrepreneurship varies within the euro-zone. Entrepreneurship is influenced by local social values as well as a variety of local economic and regulatory conditions.

The euro-zone has created "convergence on the part of the supply side of the equation which was achieved through hundreds of legislation enacted through the European Parliament. But vast differences in demand still prevail (Kaynak and Jallat, 2004, p. 7)." Within the euro-zone, convergence allows access to raw materials, but SMEs often experience problems as individually they lack buying power. *Networking is a solution*, and geographic proximity may facilitate networking.

Likewise, by providing a critical mass, *clusters allow strong joint initiatives*. In other words, *by means of clustering and networking with other firms* (that could otherwise be competitors) *competitiveness is increased*. As suggested by Miles *et al.*, "Whereas investment in the development of collegial values is intended to reduce the need for *a priori* calculation of returns from cooperative information and idea sharing, a more recent approach called *co-opetition* (simultaneous cooperation and competition) sets out to make such calculations both more explicit and accurate (2005, p. 39)." For a detailed discussion of co-opetition, see Lado *et al.* (1997).

14.2   Symbiosis

In contrast to traditional, independent entrepreneurship, we see *symbiotic networks* in which entrepreneurs benefit from working near one another in clusters, or with each other in multi-polar networks. Austria's sub-contractors — united in the form of an association — have symbiotic relationships with other firms. Likewise, Finland's network of technology and science parks promotes symbiotic entrepreneurship, as do formal networks in Ireland and elsewhere. *Clusters, like networks, facilitate access to role models, information, tacit knowledge, assistance and skills*. Clusters are not a new phenomenon; endowed with high quality clay, Saint Jean de Fos (near Montpellier) is known to have had a pottery cluster in the Middle Ages, and in the 19th century, Marshall (1890) studied the geographic dimension of industrial districts. The point being made here is that *clusters seem to be helping entrepreneurs and changing the nature of entrepreneurship across the euro-zone*. As stated by Rocha and Sternberg, "Clusters are a richer industrial dimension than industrial agglomerations, including not only spatial proximity but also inter-organisational relations. Interaction is driven... by interpersonal and associational relations among people and firms within the cluster. This interaction provides established relationships and complementary linkages, two differential mechanisms to start businesses that are not present in industrial agglomerations (2005, p. 288)." In this age of globalisation, collective efficiency in a cluster leads to international competitiveness. In other words, *entrepreneurship (formerly an individual initiative) can benefit from collective action*. Each entrepreneur benefits from others in a symbiotic relationship, i.e., symbiotic entrepreneurship.

As noted by Steinmann and Scherer, "We see an emerging post-modern world which has, not only multiple power centers, but also different and competing conceptions of 'the good life' (2003, p. 76)." In many cases, entrepreneurs opt for interdependence rather than independence. As explained by Gundolf and Jaouen (2005), entrepreneurs may find that collective actions allow their small firms to benefit from exterior resources, without heavy investments or a loss in autonomy. Whereas it used to be advantageous to compete for market share, at the expense of other firms, symbiotic entrepreneurship allows co-operating firms to enlarge the market size, with multiple firms benefiting. Such symbiotic entrepreneurship is especially useful in R&D management. Ulijn and Fayolle (2004) discussed the importance of co-operation in various European contexts. Yet, we should not expect uniformity. The euro-zone manifests horizontal networking, especially with machinery, but vertical networking in less visible in the north than in the south. As discussed in Chapter 2, Austrian entrepreneurs benefit by outsourcing; in France, large firms sub-contract to entrepreneurs. Important differences exist even within a country. As explained in Chapter 13, Madrid's electronics sector is a complex web of interdependent firms. In contrast, Catalonia has a hub-and-spoke structure, with multinationals ringed by Spanish sub-contractors.

14.3   *Observing the Trends*

It used to be that firms expanded their scope by acquiring other firms, thereby increasing their own size, albeit at a financial cost. Mergers are complex, time-consuming and costly, as they involve ownership. An alternative to vertical and horizontal integration is for firms to outsource to smaller ones. As stated by Ulijn and Brown, "Large MNCs may gain by helping small start-ups and SMEs (2004, p. 8)." Rocha and Sternberg wrote, "MNCs generate possibilities for accessing new markets and resources, acquiring new capabilities and developing international competitiveness (2005, p. 275)." We see, therefore, a win/win situation, as SMEs benefit from opportunities provided by large firms to the mutual benefit of all parties. This is the case in traditional industrial areas, such as Lombardy in Italy, as well as in Ireland's electronic sector.

Competitive pressures encourage some firms to reduce costs through outsourcing value-added functions to smaller, specialised firms. As an integral part of a network, the smaller firms may be able to specialise further, achieving even greater cost reduction and quality control, with their large customers becoming *reciprocally dependent on them*. A healthy, mutually beneficial symbiotic interdependence is then achieved. Such interdependent and communitarian relationships (Lodge and Vogel, 1987) have long characterised some non-Western business systems (Dana, 1999c) and even the indigenous Sámi economy of Finland; *such symbiotic entrepreneurship may provide a model for European firms today.*

As noted by Miles *et al.*, "Because cooperative behaviour ultimately involves the pursuit of self-interest, it requires periodic or even continual assessment by each participant of the amount of trust and commitment of the other party (1995, p. 40)."

Often, Western management puts much effort in monitoring a transaction. In co-operative circles, it is more crucial to monitor a relationship than a transaction; where a strong relationship exists, problems can always be solved (Dana, 2000b).

Europe's emerging, highly-specialised and competitive SMEs are qualitatively different from those of the 20th century. As discussed by Rocha (2004), clusters provide the synergy of geographic proximity, an inter-firm network and an organisational or institutional network. Net-worked SMEs need not be as self-sufficient or self-reliant as were the more independent firms of the past. Entrepreneurs of the future will be able to draw upon the pooled capabilities and knowledge stock of their entire cluster or network, instead of developing the required knowledge themselves. Building on such knowledge networks is a new strategic competence. The consequences of this paradigm shift from indepen-dence toward co-dependence (Acs and Yeung, 1999) or interdepen-dence are far-reaching. Entrepreneurs will have to devise new strategies to help develop and maintain *network* capabilities, in addition to their own internal competencies.

Chapter 5 showed collective actions can allow very small French firms to benefit from exterior resources, without loosing autonomy or making heavy capital investments. In other cases, the new environ-ment calls for new strategies, often involving a trade-off between inde-pendence and efficiency. What we see is that the classic, independent entrepreneur of former times is yielding to increased co-operation and networking, similar to the non-competitive relationships observed by Bianchi (1998). This includes ethnic minority networks such as those found in Austria, Belgium, Finland, France, Germany, the Netherlands and beyond, as well as the classic networks of entrepreneurs, sometimes kinship networks, as is common in Italy. In France, Italy, Portugal, Spain and elsewhere, small firms are clustering and co-operating with one another; this includes informal as well as organised clusters. As noted by Porter (1998a), clusters increase productivity in a geographic area, they drive innovation and stimulate new venture creation. Perhaps even more strikingly, small firms are teaming up with trans-national enterprises. The result is a symbiotic network. This supports the find-ings of Dana *et al.*, "The New Europe is characterised by two over-arching trends: (1) the reduced importance of the nation-state as the relevant unit around which inter-national business activity is organised and collected; and (2) the diminishing importance of the stand-alone firm as the principal unit of business competition (2005, p. 102)." There is significant co-operation among would-be competitors. In the absence of co-operation, efficiency is not maximised. Simões noted, "Many observers have pointed out the absence of a truly co-operative culture as one of the main obstacles to the competitiveness of Portuguese companies (2004, p. 24)."

In summary, geographic expansion formerly required heavy capital expenditure, while collaborative arrangements among European firms were transaction-based, terminated at the will of any party. The newer arrangements are characterised by interdependence, with each firm relying on others in a sustained, ongoing manner. When a subcontracting market is saturated, the future may hold increased success for clusters.

14.4   *Implications for Public Policy*

Entrepreneurship must be understood in the context of national development. As argued by Ring *et al.* (2005), governments have a considerable impact on entrepreneurship. It is crucial to determine the appropriate degree of regulation to enact and to enforce, such that the benefits to society exceed the costs of compliance. Mill (1869) argued that the only purpose for which power can be rightfully exercised over a member of society against his will is to prevent harm onto others. While some regulation is required to ensure order, excessive intervention is counter-productive; this was acknowledged in the Bologna Charter, the summary of a conference held in June 13–15, 2000. To benefit an economy, tax systems should reward success. McMillan explained, "Decentralised — that is, market-based — decision-making is essential for economic success (2002, p. 149)." Indeed, to be relevant, policies must be culturally sensitive. As stated by Blond and Pabst, "Only a radical decentralisation of power and money can tie the universal hopes of the European project to each particular citizen. The EU should abandon centrally imposed determinations in favour of local discernment (2005, p. 6)." Priority for governments should include the operation of visible one-stop agencies for entrepreneurs and the availability of micro-financing.

A conducive environment fosters entrepreneurship. Even SMEs that are individually weak may become internationally competitive and successful in a positive environment. Given the positive impact of clusters on entrepreneurship (Maskell and Malmberg, 1999; Piore and Sable, 1984; Pyke *et al.*, 1992), government policies should facilitate the creation of new clusters. It is important to note, however, that not all policies are transferable from one culture to another; success in one area does not guarantee success in another region, even within the euro-zone.

14.5   *Toward Future Research*

As discussed above, we see a convergence in Europe focused on macro-level issues; technology is becoming increasingly similar. Yet, at the micro-level, Europeans are maintaining cultural uniqueness, and entrepreneurship depends on cultural context. Different countries of the euro-zone have differing levels of start-ups. This can be explained by differences in the perception of opportunities for entrepreneurship, and by motivation, both culturally influenced. There are networks across the euro-zone, but those in Italy are different than those in Greece, for example. Future research might investigate the cultural causal variables behind networks. Emirbayer and Goodwin observed that researchers have "inadequately theorised the causal role of ideals, beliefs and values of the actors that strive to realise them, as a result it has neglected the cultural and symbolic moment in the very determination of social action (1994, p. 1446)." Likewise, Jagd noted that "most of network research has, in the tradition of social network theory, focused on structural aspects of networks leaving the cultural aspects of networks inadequately analysed (2005, p. 47)."

Another exciting topic for future research is the study of collective entrepreneurship, which is becoming important in France, among other places. As discussed in Chapter 5, this involves entrepreneurial individuals who enterprise together with common resources.

References

Abercrombie, Thomas J. (1995), "The Basques: Europe's First Family," *National Geographic* 188 (5), November, pp. 74–97.

Abetti, Pier A., Joyce O'Connor, Lisa M. Ehid, Joseph L. Rocco, and Barry J. Sanders (1987), "A Tale of Two Parks: Key Factors Influencing the Location Decision Process of New Entrepreneurial Companies at Rensselaer (New York State) and Plassey (Ireland) Technology Parks," in Neil C. Churchill, John A, Hornaday, Bruce A. Kirchhoff, O. Jay Krasner, and Karl H. Vesper, eds., *Frontiers of Entrepreneurship Research*, Wellesley, Massachusetts: Babson College, pp. 26–43.

Acs, Zoltan J., and Bernard Yeung (1999), "Entrepreneurial Discovery and the Global Economy," *Global Focus* 11 (3), pp. 63–71.

Adams, Harriet Chalmers (1929), "Barcelona, Pride of the Catalans," *National Geographic* 55 (3), March, pp. 373–402.

Aldrich, Howard E. (1999), *Organizations Evolving,* London: Sage.

Amatori, Franco, and Andrea Colli (2004), "Entrepreneurship: The Italian Story," in Guido Corbetta, Morton Huse, and Davide Ravasi, eds., *Crossroads of Entrepreneurship,* Boston: Kluwer Academic, pp. 243–261.

Arenius, Pia, Erkko Autio, and Anne Kovalainen (2004), *Global Entrepreneurship Monitor*, Espoo: Helsinki University of Technology.

Arenius, Pia, Erkko Autio, Anne Kovalainen, and Paul Davidson Reynolds (2001), *Global Entrepreneurship Monitor: 2001 Finnish Executive Report,* Espoo: Helsinki University of Technology.

Auster, Ellen, and Howard E. Aldrich (1984), "Small Business Vulnerability, Ethnic Enclaves and Ethnic Enterprise," in Robin Ward and Richard Jenkins, eds., *Ethnic Communities in Business: Strategies for Economic Survival*, Cambridge: Cambridge University Press, pp. 39–54.

Austrian Institute for SME Research (1996), *Barrieren für potentielle Unternehmensgründer*, Vienna: Austrian Institute for SME Research.

Bachinger, Karl (1987), "Österreich 1918–1945," in Karl Bachinger, Hildegard Hemetsberger-Koller, and Herbert Mathis, eds., *Grundriß der österreichischen Sozial- und Wirtschaftsgeschichte von 1848 bis zur Gegenwart*, Vienna: ÖBV.

Bagnasco, Arnaldo, and Marcello Messori (1975), *Tendenze dell'economia Periferica,* Turin: Editoriale Valentino.

Bamford, Julia (1987), "The Development of Small Firms, the Traditional Family and Agrarian Patterns in Italy," in Robert Goffee and Richard Scase, eds., *Entrepreneurship in Asia: The Social Processes,* London: Croom Helm, pp. 12–25.

Baptista, Rui, and Peter Swann (1998), "Do Firms in Clusters Innovate More?" *Research Policy* 27, pp. 525–540.

Barth, Fredrik, ed. (1963), *The Role of the Entrepreneur in Social Change in Northern Norway,* Bergen: Årbok for Universitetet i Bergen.

Barth, Frederik (1967), "On the Study of Social Change," *American Anthropologist* 69 (6), December, pp. 661–669.

Beach, Hugh (1990), "Comparative Systems of Reindeer Herding," in John G. Galaty and Douglas L. Johnson, eds., *The World of Pastoralism: Herding Systems in Comparative Perspective,* New York: Guildford Press, pp. 253–298.

Becattini, Giacomo (1990), "The Marshallian District as a Socio-economic Notion," in Frank Pyke, Giacomo Becattini, and Werner Sengenberger, eds., *Industrial Districts and Inter-Firm Cooperation in Italy,* Geneva: International Institute for Labour Studies, pp. 37–51.

Becattini, Giacomo (2004), *Industrial Districts: A New Approach to Industrial Change,* Cheltenham, United Kingdom: Edward Elgar.

Becattini, Giacomo, Marco Bellandi, Babi Ottati, and Fabio Sforzi (2003), *From Industrial Districts to Local Development: An Itinerary of Research,* Cheltenham, United Kingdom: Edward Elgar.

Bell, Jim, David Demick, Ian Callaghan and Aidan O'Reilly (2004), "Irish Perspectives on Developing International Entrepreneurs," in Léo Paul Dana, ed., *Handbook of Research on International Entrepreneurship,* Cheltenham, United Kingdom: Edward Elgar, pp. 499–511.

Belletante, Bernard, Nadine Levratto, and Bernard Paranque (2001), *Diversité Economique et Modes de Financement des PMEs,* Paris: L'Harmattan.

Belshaw, Cyril S. (1955), "The Cultural Milieu of the Entrepreneur: A Critical Essay," *Explorations of Entrepreneurial History* 7 (3), February, pp. 146–163.

Benoit, Bertrand (2004), "Growing Apart: 15 years after the Wall's fall, Germany's two halves diverge," *Financial Times,* Thursday, September 23, p. 11.

Bergmann, Heiko, and Rolf Sternberg (2005), "The Changing Face of Entrepreneurship in Germany — Recent Policy Changes and their Regional Implications," Paper presented at the 2nd GEM Research Conference in Hungary, May.

Bergsmo, Trym Ivar (2001), *Four Seasons with the Reindeer People,* Oslo: Pantagruel Forlag.

Berlinski, Claire (2005), "To hell with Europe!" *The Gazette* (Montreal), Sunday, June 12, p. A-17.

Beyer, Norbert, Walter Hämmerle, and Stefan Garbislander (2005), *Ein-Personen-Unternehmen in Tirol. Situation und Zukunftsperspektiven.* Tiroler regionalpolitische Studien Nr. 27; Innsbruck: Wirtschaftskammer Tirol.

Bianchi, Giuliano (1990), "Innovating in the Local Systems of Small Medium Sized Enterprises: The Experience of Tuscany," *Entrepreneurship & Regional Development* 2, pp. 57–69.

Bianchi, Giuliano (1998), "Requiem for the Third Italy? Rise and Fall of a Successful Concept," *Entrepreneurship & Regional Development* 10, pp. 93–116.

Blim, Michael L. (1992), "Small-Scale Industrialization in a Rapidly Changing World Market," in Frances Abrahamer Rothstein and Michael L. Blim, eds., *Anthropology and the Global Factory: Studies of the New Industrialization in the Late Twentieth Century*, New York: Bergin & Garvey, pp. 85–101.

Blond, Phillip, and Adrian Pabst (2005), "A Fresh Vision: Europe Needs to Think Locally," *International Herald Tribune,* Saturday, June 25, p. 6.

Boissevain, Jeremy, and Hanneke Grotenbreg (1987), "Ethnic Enterprise in the Netherlands: The Surinamese of Amsterdam," in Robert Goffee and Richard Scase, eds., *Entrepreneurship in Asia: The Social Processes*, London: Croom Helm, pp. 105–130.

Boissevain, Jeremy, and Hanneke Grotenbreg (1988), "Culture, Structure, and Ethnic Enterprise: The Surinamese of Amsterdam," in Malcolm Cross and Han Entzinger, eds., *Lost Illusions: Caribbean Minorities in Britain and the Netherlands,* London: Routledge, pp. 221–249.

Boissevain, Jeremy, and Hanneke Grotenbreg (1989), "Entrepreneurs and the Law: Self-employed Surinamese in Amsterdam," in June Starr and Jane F. Collier, eds., *History and Power in the Study of Law: New Directions in Legal Anthropology,* Ithaca: Cornell University Press, pp. 223–251.

Bolton, Bill K., and John L. Thompson (2004), *Entrepreneurs: Talent, Temperament, Technique*, 2nd edition, Oxford: Elsevier Butterworth-Heinemann.

Bonacich, Edna (1973), "A Theory of Middleman Minorities," *American Sociological Review* 38 (5), October, pp. 583–594.

Borah, Léo A. (1938), "Some Odd Pages from the Annals of the Tulip: A 'Made' Flower of Unknown Origin Took Medieval Europe by Storm and Caused a Financial Panic in the Netherlands," *National Geographic* 64 (3), September, pp. 321–344.

Bosma, Niels S., Heleen W. Stigter, and A. R. M. Wennekers (2002), *The Long Road to the Entrepreneurial Society: Global Entrepreneurship Monitor in the Netherlands*, Zoetermeer: EIM.

Bowie, Beverley M. (1959), "Building a New Austria: Looted, Pillaged, and Occupied. Eastern Austria Remains the Gay Land of Mozart and Strauss while Striding Toward Recovery," *National Geographic* 115 (2), February, pp. 172–213.

Bradley, La Verne (1947), "Scenes of Postwar Finland," *National Geographic* 92 (2), August, pp. 233–264.

Brusco, Sebastiano (1986), "Small Firms and Industrial Districts: The Experience of Italy," in David Keeble and Egbert Wever, eds., *New Firms and Regional Development in Europe,* London: Croom Helm, pp. 184–202.

Bryson, Bill (1992), "The New World of Spain," *National Geographic* 181 (4), April, pp. 3–33.

Bryson, Bill (1995), "Essence of Provence," *National Geographic* 188 (3), September, pp. 52–77.

Buckley, Peter J. (1997), "International Technology Transfer by Small and Medium-Sized Enterprises," *Small Business Economics* 9, pp. 67–78.

Buechler, Hans C., and Judith-Maria Buechler (1992), "Spanish Galician Industrialization and the Europe of 1992: A Contextual Analysis," in Frances Abrahamer Rothstein and Michael L. Blim, eds., *Anthropology and the Global Factory: Studies of the New Industrialization in the Late Twentieth Century*, New York: Bergin & Garvey, pp. 102–118.

Bundesministerium für Wirtschaft und Arbeit (2005), *Mittelstandsbericht 2002/03. Bericht über die Situation der kleinen und mittleren Unternehmungen der gewerblichen Wirtschaft* (Medium-sized businesses report 2002/03: Report about the situation of the small and medium-sized businesses of the industrial economy), Vienna: Federal Ministry of Economy and Labour.

Burgess, Philip (1999), *Human Environmental Interactions in Upper Lapland, Finland*, Rovaniemi, Finland: Arctic Centre, University of Lapland.

Burke, Andrew E., ed., (1995), *Enterprise and the Irish Economy*, Dublin: Oak Tree Press.

Cantillon, Richard (1755), *Essai sur la nature du commerce en général*, London and Paris: R. Gyles; translated (1931), by Henry Higgs, London: MacMillan and Co.

Capaldo, Guido (1997), "Entrepreneurship in Southern Italy: Empirical Evidence of Business Creation by Young Founders," *Journal of Small Business Management* 35 (3), pp. 86–92.

Cerruti, James (1979), "Belgium: One Nation Divisible," *National Geographic* 155 (3), March, pp. 314–341.

Chan, Peng S., and Robert T. Justis (1992), "Franchising in the EC: 1992 and Beyond," *Journal of Small Business Management* 30 (1), January, pp. 83–88.

Chandler, Douglas (1938), "Belgium — Europe in Miniature," *National Geographic* 73 (4), April, pp. 398–450.

Chater, Melville (1925), "Through the Back Doors of Belgium," *National Geographic* 47 (5), May, pp. 499–540.

Chater, Melville (1929), "The Danube, Highway of Races: From the Black Forest to the Black Sea, Europe's Most Important River Has Borne the Traffic of Centuries," *National Geographic* 56 (6), December, pp. 643–698.

Cherry, Robert (1990), "Middleman Minority Theories: Their Implications for Black-Jewish Relations," *The Journal of Ethnic Studies* 17 (4), Winter, pp. 117–138.

Clark, Sydney (1948), "Luxembourg, Survivor of Invasions," *National Geographic* 93 (6), June, pp. 791–810.

Clark, Sydney (1950), "Mid-Century Holland Builds Her Future," *National Geographic* 98 (6), December, pp. 747–778.

Clarke, Edward Daniel (1824a), *Travels in Various Countries of Europe Asia and Africa: Scandinavia*, Volume 9, London: T. Cadell.

Clarke, Edward Daniel (1824b), *Travels in Various Countries of Europe Asia and Africa: Scandinavia,* Volume 10, London: T. Cadell.

Cockburn, Andrew (2003), "21st Century Slaves," *National Geographic* 204 (3), September, pp. 2–25.

Coduras, Alicia, Ignacio de la Vega, Rachida Justo, and Cristina Cruz (2005), *Global Entrepreneurship Monitor Report,* Madrid: Instituto de Empresa.

Cole, Williamson E., and Bichaka Fayissa (1991), "Urban Subsistence Labor Force: Towards a Policy-oriented and Empirically Accessible Taxonomy," *World Development* 19 (7), pp. 779–789.

Collinder, Björn (1949), *The Lapps,* Princeton, New Jersey: Princeton University Press, for the American Scandinavian Foundation.

Conger, Clement E. (1948), "Portugal is Different," *National Geographic* 94 (5), November, pp. 583–622.

Conly, Robert Leslie (1970), "Luxembourg, the Quiet Fortress," *National Geographic* 138 (1), July, pp. 69–126.

Conniff, Richard (1994), "Ireland on Fast Forward," *National Geographic* 186 (3), September, pp. 2–36.

Coquery, Natacha (1997), "The Aristocratic *Hôtel* and Its Artisans in Eighteenth-century Paris: The Market Ruled by Court Society, in Geoffrey Crossick," ed., *The Artisan and the European Town, 1500–1900,* Aldershot and Brookfield, Vermont: Ashgate, pp. 92–115.

d'Iribarne, Philippe (1989), *La Logique de l'honneur: Gestion des enterprises et traditions nationales,* Paris: Editions du Seuil.

Dana, Léo-Paul (1987), "Entrepreneurship and Venture Creation — An International Comparison of Five Commonwealth Nations," *Frontiers of Entrepreneurship Research,* pp. 573–583.

Dana, Léo-Paul (1990), "Saint Martin/Sint Maarten: A Case Study of the Effects of Politics and Culture on Economic Development," *Journal of Small Business Management* 28 (4), October, pp. 91–98.

Dana, Léo-Paul (1991), "Bring in More Entrepreneurs," *Policy Options* 12 (9), November, pp. 18–19.

Dana, Léo-Paul (1992a), "A Look at Small Business in Austria," *Journal of Small Business Management* 30 (4), October, pp. 126–130.

Dana, Léo-Paul (1992b), "Entrepreneurial Education in Europe," *Journal of Education for Business* 68 (2), November–December, pp. 74–78.

Dana, Léo-Paul (1993), "An Analysis of Strategic Intervention Policy in Namibia," *Journal of Small Business Management* 31 (3), July, pp. 90–95.

Dana, Léo-Paul (1995a), "Entrepreneurship in a Remote Sub-Arctic Community: Nome, Alaska," *Entrepreneurship: Theory and Practice,* 20 (1), Fall, pp. 55–72. Reprinted in Norris Krueger, ed., *Entrepreneurship: Critical Perspectives on Business and Management,* Volume IV, London: Routledge, 2002, pp. 255–275.

Dana, Léo-Paul (1995b), "Entrepreneurship in the Basque Country: An Ethnographic Account," *Entrepreneurship, Innovation, and Change* 4 (1), March, pp. 69–76.

Dana, Léo-Paul (1996a), "Albania in the Twilight Zone: The *Perseritje* Model and its Impact on Small Business," *Journal of Small Business Management* 24 (1), January, pp. 64–70.

Dana, Léo-Paul (1996b), "Influence du Facteur Culturel sur la Très Petite Entreprise à Strasbourg," *Journal of Small Business & Entrepreneurship* 13 (2), Summer, pp. 81–94.

Dana, Léo-Paul (1997), "The Origins of Self-Employment," *Canadian Journal of Administrative Sciences/Revue Canadienne des Sciences de l'Administration* 14 (1), April, pp. 99–104.

Dana, Léo-Paul (1998), "Waiting for Direction in the Former Yugoslav Republic of Macedonia (FYROM)," *Journal of Small Business Management* 36 (2), April, pp. 62–67.

Dana, Léo-Paul (1999a) "Bulgaria at the Crossroads of Entrepreneurship," *Journal of Euromarketing* 8 (4), December, pp. 27–50.

Dana, Léo-Paul (1999b), "Business and Entrepreneurship in Bosnia-Herzegovina," *Journal of Business & Entrepreneurship* 11 (2), October, pp. 105–118.

Dana, Léo-Paul (1999c), *Entrepreneurship in Pacific Asia,* Singapore, London and Hong Kong: World Scientific.

Dana, Léo-Paul (1999d), "Preserving Culture through Small Business: Government Support for Artisans and Craftsmen in Greece," *Journal of Small Business Management* 37 (1), January, pp. 90–92.

Dana, Léo-Paul (1999e), "The Social Cost of Tourism: A Case Study of Ios," *Cornell Quarterly* 40 (4), August, pp. 60–63.

Dana, Léo-Paul (2000a), *Economies of the Eastern Mediterranean Region: Economic Miracles in the Making,* Singapore, London and Hong Kong: World Scientific.

Dana, Léo-Paul (2000b), "International Management: Culture is of the essence in Asia," *Financial Times,* Mastering Management Special Section, November 27, pp. 12–13.

Dana, Léo-Paul (2000c), "The Hare and the Tortoise of Former Czechoslovakia: Small Business in the Czech and Slovak Republics," *European Business Review* 12 (6), November, pp. 337–343.

Dana, Léo-Paul (2002), "Entrepreneurship & Public Policy in Gibraltar," *International Journal of Entrepreneurship and Innovation Management* 2 (1), pp. 38–42.

Dana, Léo-Paul (2005a), "Sheep Farm in the Pyrenees," in Timothy S. Hatten, *Small Business Management: Entrepreneurship & Beyond,* 3rd edition, Boston: Houghton Mifflin, pp. 351–352.

Dana, Léo-Paul (2005b), *When Economies Change Hands: A Survey of Entrepreneurship in the Emerging Markets of Europe from the Balkans to the Baltic States,* Binghamton: Haworth.

Dana, Léo-Paul, and Robert Brent Anderson, eds., (in press), *Indigenous Entrepreneurship*, Cheltenham, United Kingdom: Edward Elgar.

Dana, Léo-Paul, Mark B. Bajramovic, and Richard W. Wright (2005), "Chapter 5: A New Paradigm of Multipolar Competition and Its Implications for Entrepreneurship in Europe," in Alain Fayolle, Paula Kyrö, and Jan Ulijn, eds., *Entrepreneurship Research in Europe: Outcomes and Perspectives,* Cheltenham, United Kingdom: Edward Elgar, pp. 102–117.

Dana, Léo-Paul, and Teresa E. Dana (2003), "Innovative Policies for Entrepreneurship: The Principality of Liechtenstein & the Grand Duchy of Luxembourg," *International Journal of Entrepreneurship and Innovation Management* 3 (3), June, pp. 295–302.

Dana, Léo-Paul, Mary Han, Vanessa Ratten, and Isabell Welpe, eds., (forthcoming), *A Theory of Internationalisation for European Entrepreneurship,* Cheltenham, United Kingdom: Edward Elgar.

Dana, Léo-Paul, Len Korot, and George Tovstiga (2000), "Toward a Transnational Techno-culture: An Empirical Investigation of Knowledge Management," in Hamid Etemad and Richard Wright, eds., *Globalization and Entrepreneurship: Policy and Strategy Perspectives,* Cheltenham, United Kingdom: Edward Elgar, pp. 183–204.

Dana, Teresa E., and Liisa Remes (2005), "Entrepreneurship among the Sámi People of Finland," *Journal of Small Business & Entrepreneurship* 18 (2), Spring, pp. 189–200.

Davenport, William (1974), "Amiable Amsterdam," *National Geographic* 145 (5), May, pp. 682–705.

Davenport, William (1980), "Bordeaux: Fine Wines and Fiery Gascons," *National Geographic* 158 (2), August, pp. 233–259.

De Clercq, Dirk, Sophie Manigart, Bart Clarysse, Hans Crijns, Mathieu de Sutter, and Frank Verzele (2002), *The Global Entrepreneurship Monitor Executive Report for Belgium 2003,* Ghent: Ghent University.

De Clercq, Dirk, Sophie Manigart, Hans Crijns, Bart Clarysse, Frank Verzele, and David Zegers (2004), *The Global Entrepreneurship Monitor Executive Report for Belgium & Wallonia 2003,* Ghent: Ghent University.

Del Monte, Alfredo, and Domenico Scalera (2001) "The Life-duration of Small Firms Born with a Start-up Programme: Evidence from Italy," *Regional Studies* 35 (1), pp. 11–21.

Dimitratos, Pavlos, and Spyros Lioukas (2004), "Greek Perspectives of International Entrepreneurship," in Léo-Paul Dana, ed., *Handbook of Research on International Entrepreneurship,* Cheltenham, United Kingdom: Edward Elgar, pp. 455–480.

Ducros, Christine, Jean-Yves Guérin, and Brunot Jacquot (2004), "Tous Entrepreneurs!" *Le Figaro Entreprises*, September 13, pp. 18–23.

Edwards, Walter Meayers (1951), "France's Past Lives in Languedoc," *National Geographic* 100 (1), July, pp. 1–43.

Ehmer, Josef (1997), "Worlds of Mobility: Migration Patterns of Viennese Artisans in the Eighteenth Century," in Geoffrey Crossick, ed., *The Artisan and the European Town, 1500–1900,* Aldershot and Brookfield, Vermont: Ashgate, pp. 172–199.

El-Namaki, M. S. S. (1992), "Europe After Integration: Existing and Prospective Propensities to Enterprise in Four EC Countries at Different Stages of Economic Growth," *Entrepreneurship, Innovation, and Change* 1 (1), March, pp. 87–96.

Ellis, William S. (1984), "Surviving, Italian Style," *National Geographic* 165 (2), February, pp. 185–209.

Emirbayer, Mustafa, and Jeff Goodwin (1994), "Network Analysis, Culture, and the Problem of Agency," *American Journal of Sociology* 99 (6), pp. 1411–1454.

Enterprise Strategy Group (2004), *Ahead of the Curve: Ireland's Place in the Global Economy,* Dublin: Forfás.

Farmer, Richard N., and Barry M. Richman (1965), *Comparative Management and Economic Progress,* Homewood, Illinois: Richard D. Irwin.

Fayolle, Alain (2000), "L'enseignement de l'entrepreneuriat dans le Système Educatif Supérieur Français: Un Regard sur la Situation Actuelle," *Gestion 2000* (3), pp. 77–95.

Fayolle, Alain (2004), "French Perspectives of International Entrepreneurship," in Léo-Paul Dana, ed., *Handbook of Research on International Entrepreneurship,* Cheltenham, United Kingdom: Edward Elgar, pp. 431–454.

Fayolle, Alain, Paula Kyrö, and Jan Ulijn (2005), "The Entrepreneurship Debate in Europe: A Matter of History and Culture?" in Alain Fayolle, Paula Kyrö, and Jan Ulijn, eds., *Entrepreneurship Research in Europe: Outcomes and Perspectives,* Cheltenham, United Kingdom: Edward Elgar, pp. 1–31.

Fehrenbach, Silke, and Maria Lauxen-Ulbrich (2006), "A Gender View on Self-Employment in Germany," *International Journal of Entrepreneurship and Small Business* 3.

Fertala, Nikolinka (2003), "Immigrants' Propensity to Self-Employment in Germany," *Journal of Transforming Societies and Economies* 4 (38), pp. 30–40.

Fisher, Clyde (1939), "The Nomads of Arctic Lapland: Mysterious Little People of a Land of the Midnight Sun Live Off the Country above the Arctic Circle," *National Geographic* 76 (5), November, pp. 641–676.

Fitzsimons, Paula, and Colm O'Gorman (2004), *The Irish Report: How Entrepreneurial is Ireland?* Dublin: University College.

Fontaine, Pascal (2000), *A New Idea for Europe: The Schuman Declaration 1950–2000,* Luxembourg: Office for Official Publications of the European Communities.

Ford, Richard (1929), "Seville, More Spanish than Spain: The City of the Ibero-American Exposition, Which Opens This Spring, Presents a Tapestry of Many Ages and of Nations Old and New," *National Geographic* 55 (3), March, pp. 273–310.

Fotopoulos, Georgios, and Nigel Spence (1998), "Accounting for Net Entry into Greek Manufacturing by Establishments of Varying Size," *Small Business Economics* 11, pp. 125–144.

Frank, Hermann, Alexander Kessler, Christian Korunka, and Manfred Lueger (2002), *Von der Gründungsidee zum Unternehmenserfolg. Eine empirische Analyse von Entwicklungsverläufen österreichischer Gründungen. Veröffentlichungen zur Mittelstandspolitik 6*; Vienna: Federal Ministry of Economics and Labour of the Republic of Austria.

Fraser, Lindley M. (1937), *Economic Thought and Language*, London: A & C Black.

Friedrichs, Christopher R. (1997), "Artisans and Urban Politics in Seventeenth-century Germany," in Geoffrey Crossick, ed., *The Artisan and the European Town, 1500–1900,* Aldershot and Brookfield, Vermont: Ashgate, pp. 41–55.

Fritsch, Michael, and Pamela Müller (2004) "Effects of New Business Formation on Regional Development over Time," *Regional Studies* (38) 8, pp. 961–976.

Fritsch, Michael, and Jürgen Schmude (forthcoming), *Entrepreneurship in the Region*, Boston: Springer.

Gartner, William B. (1989), "Some Suggestions for Research on Entrepreneurial Traits and Characteristics," *Entrepreneurship: Theory & Practice* 14, pp. 27–37.

Getzner, Michael, Gottfried Haber, and Erich Schwarz (2004), *Gesamtwirtschaftliche Effekte der Unternehmensgründungen in Österreich 2003. Forschungsbericht. Version 2.13.* (Macroeconomic effects of enterprise foundations in Austria in 2003. Survey-report), Klagenfurt: Institut für Wirtschaftwissenschaften Universität Klagenfurt.

Gibbons, Patrick T., and Tony O'Connor (2005), "Influences on Strategic Planning Processes among Irish SMEs," *Journal of Small Business Management* 43 (2), pp. 170–186.

Glassey, Frank P. S. (1925), "Helsingfors — A Contrast in Light and Shade," *National Geographic* 47 (5), May, pp. 597–612.

Glassman, Ulrich, and Helmut Voelzkow (2001), "The Governance of Local Economies in Germany," in Colin Crouch, Patrick Le Galès, Carlo Trigilia, and Helmut Voelzkow, eds., *Local Production Systems in Europe, Rise or Demise?* Oxford, United Kingdom: Oxford University Press, pp. 79–116.

Graves, William (1967), "The Rhine," *National Geographic* 131 (4), April, pp. 449–499.

Graves, William (1968), "Finland: Plucky Neighbor of Soviet Russia," *National Geographic* 133 (5), May, pp. 587–629.

Graves, William (1980), "After an Empire... Portugal," *National Geographic* 158 (6), December, pp. 804–831.

Grichnik, Dietmar, and Robert D. Hisrich (2005), "Entrepreneurship Education needs Arising from Entrepreneurial Profiles in Unified Germany — An International Comparison," *Piccola Impresa / Small Business Management* 3, pp. 101–127.

Grimond, John (1990), "Italy Survey," insert in *The Economist*, May 26.

Grin, John, Francisca Felix, Bram Bos, and Sierk Spoelstra (2004), "Practices for Reflexive Design: Lessons from a Dutch Programme on Sustainable Agriculture," *International Journal of Foresight and Innovation Policy* 1 (1/2), pp. 126–149.

Groen, Aard, Jan Ulijn, and Alain Fayolle (2006), "Educational Diversity in Technology Entrepreneurship: Some experiences from France and the Netherlands," *International Journal of Entrepreneurship and Small Business* 3.

Grosvenor, Gilbert M., and Charles Neave (1954), "Helping Holland Rebuild Her Land," *National Geographic* 106 (3), September, pp. 365–413.

Gundolf, Katherine, and Annabelle Jaouen (2005), "Patterns and Coordination of Collective Action in Small and Very Small Business: The Case of a Tourist Village in the Pyrenees," *International Journal of Entrepreneurship and Small Business* 2 (4), pp. 392–403.

Hau, Michel, and Nicolas Stoskopf (2005), *Les Dynasties Alsaciennes: du XVIIe siècle à nos jours,* Paris: Perrin.

Haberfellner, Regina (2003), "Austria: Still a Highly Regulated Economy," in Robert Kloosterman and Jan Rath, eds., *Immigrant Entrepreneurs: Venturing Abroad in the Age of Globalization,* Oxford: Berg, pp. 213–232.

Haetta, Odd Mathis (1996), *The Sami: An Indigenous People of the Arctic,* translated by Ole Petter Gurholt, Vaasa, Finland: Davvi Girji.

Harrison, Bennett (1992), "Industrial Districts: Old Wine in New Bottles?" *Regional Studies* 26, pp. 469–483.

Henry, Thomas R. (1945), "War's Wake in the Rhineland," *National Geographic* 88 (1), July, pp. 1–32.

Henry, Thomas R. (1946), "Holland Rises from War and Water," *National Geographic* 89 (2), February, pp. 237–260.

Henschel, Thomas (2006), "Risk Management Practices in German SMEs: An Empirical Investigation," *International Journal of Entrepreneurship and Small Business* 3.

Hofstede, Geert (1980), *Culture's Consequences: International Differences in Work-Related Values,* Beverly Hills, California: Sage.

Hosmer, Dorothy (1941), "Rhodes, and Italy's Aegean Islands," *National Geographic* 79 (4), April, pp. 449–480.

Hume, Edgar Erskine (1949), "Italy Smiles Again," *National Geographic* 95 (6), June, pp. 693–732.

Hume, Edgar Erskine (1951), "The Palio of Siena," *National Geographic* 100 (2), August, pp. 231–244.

Hunnisett, Stanley F., and Jukka Pennanen (1991), "Saami, Gypsies, Indians, and Immigrants," *Ethnos* 1991 (3–4), pp. 210–223.

Huntington, Samuel P. (1993), "The Clash of Civilization," *Foreign Affairs* 72 (3), pp. 22–49.

Huntington, Samuel P. (1996), *The Clash of Civilization and the Remaking of World Order*, New York: Simon and Schuster.

Hutchison, Isobel Wylie (1951), "A Stroll to Venice," *National Geographic* 100 (3), September, pp. 378–410.

Ingold, Tim (1976), *The Skolt Lapps Today,* Cambridge: Cambridge University Press.

Jääskö, Outi (1999), "Women's Position in Reindeer Herding Economy: An Environmental Factor," in Ludger Müller-Wille, ed., *Human Environmental Interactions: Issues and Concerns in Upper Lapland, Finland*, Rovaniemi: Arctic Centre, University of Lapland, pp. 35–40.

Jagd, Søren (2005), "The 'Network Ethic' and the New Spirit of Capitalism in French Sociology of Capitalism," in Sokratis M. Koniordos, ed., *Networks, Trust and Social Capital: Theoretical and Empirical Investigations from Europe*, Aldershot,United Kingdom: Ashgate, pp. 47–69.

Javetski, Bill, and John Templeman (1990), "One Germany: The whole European equation has changed," *Business Week*, April 2, pp. 47–49.

Jennings, Gary (1974), "Bavaria: Mod, Medieval — and Bewitching," *National Geographic* 145 (3), March, pp. 409–431.

Jernsletten, Johnny-Léo L., and Konstantin Klokov (2002), *Sustainable Reindeer Husbandry*, Tromsø: University of Tromsø Centre for Saami Studies.

Johansson, Edvard (2000), "Self-employment and the Predicted Earning Differential — Evidence from Finland," *Finnish Economic Papers* 13 (1), Spring, pp. 45–55.

Judge, Joseph (1972), "Venice Fights for Life," *National Geographic* 142 (5), November, pp. 591–631.

Kanein, Werner, and Günter Renner (1988), *Ausländerrecht, Kommentar*, 4th edition, Munich: C. H. Beck.

Kanellopoulos, Charal C. (1987), "Greek-American Entrepreneurship: Traits, Motives, Behavior and Values," in Neil C. Churchill, John A. Hornaday, Bruce A. Kirchhoff, O. J. Krasner, and Karl H. Vesper, eds., *Frontiers of Entrepreneurship Research*, Wellesley, Massachusetts: Babson College, pp. 24–25.

Kantis, Hugo (2005), "The Emergence of Dynamic Ventures in Latin America, Southern Europe and East Asia: An International Comparison," *International Journal of Entrepreneurship and Small Business* 2 (1), pp. 34–56.

Kaynak, Erdener, and Frédéric Jallat (2004), "Marketing in Western Europe: A Monolith or a Multidimensional Market," *Journal of Euromarketing* 14 (1–2), pp. 1–14.

Kemp, Ron, and Clemens Lutz (2006), "Perceived Barriers to Entry: Is There Any Difference between Small, Medium-Sized and Large Companies?" *International Journal of Entrepreneurship and Small Business*, 3.

Kerbey, McFall (1940), "Behind Netherlands Sea Ramparts," *National Geographic* 77 (2), February, pp. 255–290.

Kihn, W. Langdon (1936), "A Palette from Spain," *National Geographic* 69 (3), March, pp. 407–440.

Klandt, Heinz (1987), "Trends in Small Business Start-up in West Germany," in Robert Goffee and Richard Scase, eds., *Entrepreneurship in Europe: The Social Processes*, London: Croom Helm, pp. 26–38.

Klandt, Heinz (1997), "State of the Art of Entrepreneurship and SME Research and Education in Germany," in Hans Landström, Hermann Frank, and

Malaise, N. (1988), *Conditions de travail et petites et moyennes entreprises,* Dublin: Fondation européenne pour l'amélioration des conditions de vie et de travail.

Mandl, Irene (2004), *Business Transfers and Successions in Austria,* Vienna: Austrian Institute for SME Research.

Marden, Luis (1955), "Bruges, the City the Sea Forgot: Belgium's Chief Port and World-trade Center in Medieval Days Relives Its Past in Brilliant, Reverent Pageantry," *National Geographic* 107 (5), May, pp. 631–665.

Marsh, Peter (2004), "Customisation: Mass-produced for Individual Tastes," *Financial Times,* April 22, p. 8.

Marshall, Alfred (1890), *Principles of Economics: An Introductory Text,* London: Macmillan.

Maskell Peter and Anders Malmberg (1999), "Localised Learning and Industrial Competitiveness," *Cambridge Journal of Economics* 23, pp. 167–185.

Mauco, Georges (1932), *Les Etrangers en France: Etude Géographique sur leur Rôle dans l'activité Economique,* Paris: Armand Collin.

Mayer, Nonna (1987), "Small Business and Social Mobility in France," in Robert Goffee and Richard Scase, eds., *Entrepreneurship in Asia: The Social Processes,* London: Croom Helm, pp. 39–59.

McBride, Harry A. (1929), "On the Bypaths of Spain," *National Geographic* 55 (3), March, pp. 311–372.

McBride, Harry A. (1931), "Pursuing Spanish Bypaths Northwest of Madrid," *National Geographic* 59 (1), January, pp. 121–130.

McBride, Ruth Q. (1936), "Turbulent Spain," *National Geographic* 70 (4), October, pp. 397–427.

McCarry, John (1992), "Milan: Where Italy gets down to business," *National Geographic* 182 (6), December, pp. 90–122.

McDonald, Michael Dwyer, and Frank Wendt (1994), "Italy's Black Economy: Corporate Indiscretion," *Management Decision* 32 (3), pp. 49–52.

McDowell, Bart (1965), "The Changing Face of Old Spain," *National Geographic* 127 (3), March, pp. 291–339.

McDowell, Bart (1986), "The Dutch Treat," *National Geographic* 170 (4), October, pp. 501–525.

McGrath, Rita Gunter, Ian C. MacMillan, and Sari Scheinberg (1992), "Elitists, Risk-Takers, and Rugged Individualists? An Exploratory Analysis of Cultural Differences Between Entrepreneurs and Non-Entrepreneurs," *Journal of Business Venturing* 7, pp. 115–135.

McMillan, John (2002), *Reinventing the Bazaar: The Natural History of Markets,* New York: W. W. Norton & Co.

Meulemans, Dirk (2000), "Developing Startpunt, a Business Incubator for the Social Economy," in Dirk Deschoolmeester, Daniel De Steur, Kathy Gillis, and Tom Schamp, eds., *Entrepreneurship Under Difficult Circumstances,* Seminar Proceedings of the 30th European Small Business Seminar, Gent, Belgium, September 20–22, pp. 95–105.

Miles, Marc A., Edwin J. Feulner, and Mary Anastasia O'Grady (2005), *2005 Index of Economic Freedom,* Washington, DC: The Heritage Foundation.

Miles, Raymond E., Grant Miles, and Charles C. Snow (2005), *Collaborative Entrepreneurship: How Communities of Networked Firms Innovate to Create Economic Wealth,* Stanford: Stanford University Press.

Mill, John Stuart (1869), *On Liberty,* London: Longman, Roberts and Green.

Miller, Helen Hill (1960), "Rotterdam — Reborn from Ruins," *National Geographic* 118 (4), October, pp. 526–553.

Minniti, Maria (2005), "Self-employment and Organization Creation: The Case of Italy," *Global Business and Economic Review.*

Minniti, Maria, and Patrizia Venturelli (2000), *Global Entrepreneurship Monitor National Assessment: Italy 2000 Executive Report,* Wellesley: Babson College.

Mitchell, Carleton (1970), "Capri, Italy's Enchanted Rock," *National Geographic* 137 (6), June, pp. 795–809.

Moore, W. Robert (1938), "Castles and Progress in Portugal," *National Geographic* 73 (2), February, pp. 133–188.

Moore, W. Robert (1943), "The Coasts of Normandy and Brittany," *National Geographic* 84 (2), August, pp. 205–224.

Mugler, Josef (1998), *Betriebswirtschaftslehre der Klein- und Mittelbetriebe*, Vienna: Springer.

Mulhern, Alan (1995), "The SME Sector in Europe: A Broad Perspective," *Journal of Small Business Management* 33 (3), July, pp. 83–87.

Müller-Wille, Ludger (1978), "Cost Analysis of Modern Hunting Among the Inuit of the Canadian Central Arctic," *Polar Geography* 2 (2), pp. 104–114.

Müller-Wille, Ludger (1987), "Indigenous People, Land-use Conflicts, and Economic Development in Circumpolar Lands," *Arctic and Alpine Research* 19 (4), pp. 351–356.

Müller-Wille, Ludger, and Pertti J. Pelto (1971), "Technological Change and Its Impact in Arctic Regions: Lapps Introduce Snowmobiles into Reindeer Herding, *Polarforschung* 41, pp. 142–148.

Mumford, Lewis (1938), *The Culture of Cities,* New York: Harcourt Brace Jovanovich.

Musgrave, Elizabeth (1997), "Women and the Craft Guilds in Eighteenth-century Nantes," in Geoffrey Crossick, ed., *The Artisan and the European Town, 1500–1900,* Aldershot and Brookfield, Vermont: Ashgate, pp. 151–171.

Ní Bhrádaigh, Emer (in press), "Entrepreneurship in the Gaeltachtaí of Ireland," in Léo-Paul Dana and Robert Brent Anderson, eds., *Indigenous Entrepreneurship,* Cheltenham, United Kingdom: Edward Elgar.

Nijkamp, Peter, Cher Guldemond, and Hugo Teelen (2004), "The Importance of Venture Capital for High-tech Development Experiences from the Netherlands and Israel," *International Journal of Entrepreneurship and Innovation Management* 4 (1), pp. 41–49.

Niskanen, Kirst (2001), "Theoretical Issues: Gender Economics in Action: Rural Women's Economic Citizenship in Finland during the Twentieth Century," *Journal of Women's History* 13 (2), Summer, pp. 132–152.

Nolan, John E. H. (1954), "In the Land of the Basques," *National Geographic* 105 (2), February, pp. 147–187.

Nothdurft, William E. (1992), *Going Global: How Europe Helps Small Firms Export*, Washington, DC: Brookings Institution.

Obrecht, Jean-Jacques (2002), "The Public System of Incubators in France," in Peter C. van der Sijde, Birgit Wirsing, Rudi Cluyvers, and Annemarie Ridder, eds., *New Concepts for Academic Entrepreneurship*, Twente: Twente University Press.

Obrecht, Jean-Jacques (2005), "L'entrepreneuriat International: Un rhizome vigoureux dans un terrain nouveau," *Les Sciences de Gestion au Cœur du Développement*, Actes du Colloque International INSCAE, Antananarivo, Madagascar, November 2–4.

Ohlson, Birger (1960), "Settlement and Economic Life in Enotekiö — A Parish in the Extreme North of Finland," *Fennia* 84, pp. 21–46.

Olson, Alma Luise (1938), "The Farthest-North Republic: Olympic Games and Arctic Flying Bring Sequestered Finland into New Focus of World Attention," *National Geographic* 74 (4), October, pp. 499–534.

Paché, Gilles (1996), "The Small Producer in the French Food Distribution Channel," *Journal of Small Business Management* 34 (2), April, pp. 84–88.

Padmore, Tim, and Hervey Gibson (1997), "Modelling Systems of Innovation: A Framework for Industrial Cluster Analysis in Regions," *Research Policy* 26, pp. 625–641.

Paine, Robert (1964), "Herding and Husbandry: Two Basic Distinctions in the Analysis of Reindeer Management," *Folk* 6 (1), pp. 83–88.

Paine, Robert (1994), *Herds of the Tundra: A Portrait of Saami Reindeer Pastoralism*, Washington, DC, and London: Smithsonian Institution Press.

Pang, Ching Lin (2003), "Belgium: From Proletarians to Proteans," in Robert Kloosterman and Jan Rath, eds., *Immigrant Entrepreneurs: Venturing Abroad in the Age of Globalization*, Oxford: Berg, pp. 195–212.

Pascal, Blaise (1701), *Pensées sur la religion, et sur quelques autres sujets. Augmentée de beaucoup de pensées, de la vie de l'auteur, & de quelques dissertations*, Amsterdam: Pierre Mortier.

Patric, John (1940), "Italy, from Roman Ruins to Radio," *National Geographic* 77 (3), March, pp. 347–394.

Pattisson, Naomi, and Adam Lindgreen (2004), "Success and Failures in the Dairy Industry: South West England and North West France," *British Food Journal* 106 (6), pp. 422–435.

Peet, John (2002), "Model Makers: A Survey of the Netherlands," insert in *The Economist*, May 4.

Peet, John (2005), "Addio, Dolce Vita," insert in *The Economist*, November 26.

Pelto, Pertti Juho, and Ludger Müller-Wille (1972/3), "Reindeer Herding and Snow-mobiles: Aspects of a Technological Revolution," *Folk* 14–15, pp. 119–144.

Pennewiss, Sandra (2004), "The Old Man and the Sea: A Field Study of Change in the Greek Fishing Industry Based on Interviews with Fishermen on the Island of Santorini," *International Journal of Entrepreneurship & Small Business* 1 (1/2), pp. 206–210.

Pereira, Elisabeth T., and António Jorge Fernandes (2006), "Clusters Development as a Factor of Competitive Advantage," *International Journal of Entrepreneurship and Small Business* 3.

Pereira, Elisabeth T., António Jorge Fernandes, and Henrique Manuel Morais Diz (2004), "Evolutionary Economics: Application to the Case of Ceramics Industry in the Portuguese District of Aveiro," presented at the conference, New Economic Windows 2004: Complexity Hints for Economic Policy, University of Salerno, Salerno, Italy, September.

Perier, Mme (1842), *Pensées de Pascal, Précédées de sa Vie par Mme Perier, sa Soeur, Suivies d'un Choix des Pensées de Nicole, et son Traité de la Paix avec les Hommes,* Paris: Librairie de Firmin Didot Frères, Imprimeur de l'Institut.

Peterson, Rein, and Mari Peterson (1981), "The Impact of Economic Regulation and Paperwork," *Regulation Reference Working Paper Series,* Ottawa, Canada: Economic Council of Canada.

Pichler, J. Hanns, and Walter Bornett (2005), "Wirtschaftliche Bedeutung der kleinen und mittleren Unternehmen (KMU) in Österreich," in Reinbert Schauer, Norbert Kailer, and Birgit Norbert, eds., *Mittelständische Unternehmen;* Linz, Austria: Trauner.

Pickerell, James H. (1968), "Dory on the Banks: A Day in the Life of a Portuguese Fisherman," *National Geographic* 133 (4), April, pp. 573–583.

Piore, Michael J., and Charles F. Sabel (1984), *The Second Industrial Divide,* New York: Basic Books.

Porter, Michael E. (1990), *The Competitive Advantage of Nations,* New York: Free Press.

Porter, Michael E. (1998a), "Clusters and the New Economics of Competition," *Harvard Business Review* 76 (6), November–December, pp. 77–90.

Porter, Michael E. (1998b), *On Competition,* Boston, Massachusetts: Harvard Business School Press.

Potts, Neil (2000), "Will the Single European Market Make Us all Richer and Happier?" *European Business Review* 12 (6), pp. 332–336.

Putman, John J. (1977), "West Germany: Continuing Miracle," *National Geographic* 152 (2), August, pp. 149–181.

Putman, John J. (1981), "A New Day for Ireland," *National Geographic* 159 (4), April, pp. 442–469.

Putman, John J. (1986), "Madrid: The Change in Spain," *National Geographic* 169 (2), February, pp. 142–181.

Pyke, Frank, Giacomo Becattini, and Werner Sengenberger (1992), *Industrial Districts and Inter-firm Co-operation in Italy,* Geneva: International Labour Organisation.

Rabellotti, Roberta (1995), "Is There an 'Industrial District Model'? Footwear Districts in Italy and Mexico Compared," *World Development* 23, pp. 29–41.

Raes, Stephan (2000), "Chapter 1: Regionalization in a Globalizing World: The Emergence of Clothing Sweatshops in the European Union," in Jan Rath, ed., *Immigrant Businesses: The Economic, Political and Social Environment,* Houndmills, Basingstoke, Hampshire: Macmillan, pp. 20–36.

Rainnie, Al, and Michael Scott (1986), "Industrial Relations in the Small Firm," in James Curran, John Stanworth, and David Watkins, eds., *The Survival of the Small Firm,* Aldershot, United Kingdom: Gower, pp. 42–60.

Rama, Ruth, and Ascension Calatrava (2002), "The Advantages of Clustering: The Case of Spanish Electronics Subcontractors," *International Journal of Technology Management* 24 (7–8), pp. 764–791.

Rama, Ruth, Deron Ferguson, and Ana Melero (2003), "Subcontracting Networks in Industrial Districts: The Electronics Industries of Madrid," *Regional Studies* 37 (1), pp. 71–88.

Range, Peter Ross (2003), "Corsica: France's Island Paradox," *National Geographic* 203 (4), April, pp. 56–75.

Rath, Jan (2002), "Do Immigrant Entrepreneurs Play the Game of Ethnic Musical Stairs? A Critique of Waldinger's Model of Immigrant Incorporation," in Anthony M. Messina, ed., *West European Immigration and Immigrant Policy in the New Century*, Westport, Connecticut: Praeger, pp. 141–159.

Rath, Jan (2003), "Undressing the Garment Industry: Immigrant Entrepreneurship in Seven Cities," in Jeffrey G. Reitz, ed., *Host Societies and the Reception of Immigrants,* La Jolla, California: Centre for Comparative Immigration Studies, pp. 253–286.

Rath, Jan and Robert Kloosterman (2003), "The Netherlands: A Dutch Treat," in Robert Kloosterman and Jan Rath, eds., *Immigrant Entrepreneurs: Venturing Abroad in the Age of Globalization,* Oxford: Berg, pp. 123–146.

Reynolds, Paul Davidson (1997), "New and Small Firms in Expanding Markets," *Small Business Economics* 9 (1), pp. 79–84.

Rice, William Gorham (1925), "The Singing Towers of Holland and Belgium," *National Geographic* 47 (3), March, pp. 357–376.

Ring, Peter Smith, Gregory A. Bigley, Thomas D'Aunno, and Tarun Khanna (2005), "Perspectives on *How* Governments Matter," *Academy of Management Review* 30 (2), April, pp. 308–320.

Riseth, Jan Åge (2003), "Sami Reindeer Management in Norway: Modernization Challenges and Conflicting Strategies. Reflections Upon the Co-management Alternative," in Svein Jentoft, Henry Minde, and Ragnar Nilsen, eds., *Indigenous Peoples: Resource Management and Global Rights,* Delft, The Netherlands: Eburon Academic, pp. 229–247.

Rocha, Hector O. (2004), "Entrepreneurship and Development: The Role of Clusters. A Literature Review," *Small Business Economics* 23 (5), pp. 363–400.

Rocha, Hector O., and Rolf Sternberg (2005), "Entrepreneurship: The Role of Clusters. Theoretical Perspectives and Empirical Evidence from Germany," *Small Business Economics* 24 (3), pp. 267–292.

Routamaa, Vesa, and Katri Mäki-Tarkka (2005), "The Case of Finland," in Anders Lundström, ed., *Creating Opportunities for Young Entrepreneurship: Nordic Examples and Experiences*, Örebro: Swedish Foundation for Small Business Research, pp. 113–175.

Ruong, Israel (1937), *Geographica: Fjällapparna I Jukkasjärvi Socken*, Uppsala, Sweden: Appelbergs Boktryckeriaktiebolag.

Ruotsala, Helena (1999), "The Reindeer Herder's Environment," in Ludger Müller-Wille, ed., *Human Environmental Interactions: Issues and Concerns in Upper Lapland, Finland*, Rovaniemi: Arctic Centre, University of Lapland, pp. 41–47.

Santayana, George (1905), *The Life of Reason*, New York: Charles Scribner's Sons.

Savitt, Ronald (1998), "This Thing I Call Europe," *International Marketing Review* 15 (6), pp. 444–447.

Say, Jean Baptiste (1816), *Catechism of Political Economy: Or, Familiar Conversations of the Manner in Which Wealth is Produced, Distributed, and Consumed by Society*, London: Sherwood.

Scase, Richard (1980), *The State in Western Europe*, London: Croom Helm.

Scase, Richard, and Robert Goffee (1987), *The Real World of the Small Business Owner*, London: Croom Helm.

Scheinberg, Sari, and Ian C. MacMillan (1988), "An 11 Country Study of Motivations to Start a Business," *Frontiers of Entrepreneurship Research*, Wellesley, Massachusetts: Babson College, pp. 669–687.

Schmidt, Karl-Heinz (1992), *Internationalization, Subcontracting and Firm-Size*, Paderborn: Universität — Gesamthochschule Paderborn.

Schmidt, Karl-Heinz (1999), *State and Industrialization During the 19th Century*, Paderborn: Universität Paderborn, Fachbereich Wirtschaftswißenschaftn.

Schot, Johan W. (1988), "The Usefulness of Evolutionary Models for Explaining Innovation: The Case of the Netherlands in the Nineteenth Century," *History and Technology* 14, pp. 173–200.

Schumpeter, Joseph A. (1934), *The Theory of Economic Development: An Inquiry into Profits, Capital, Credit, Interest, and the Business Cycle*, translated by Redvers Opie, Cambridge, Massachusetts: Harvard University Press.

Schwarz, Erich J., and Eva Grieshuber (2003): *Vom Gründungs-zum Jungunternehmen*; Vienna and New York: Springer.

Scofield, John (1969), "The Friendly Irish," *National Geographic* 136 (3), September, pp. 354–391.

Severy, Merle (1989), "The Great Revolution," *National Geographic* 176 (1), July, pp. 18–49.

Sheats, Dorothea (1951), "I Walked Some Irish Miles," *National Geographic* 99 (5), May, pp. 653–678

Shor, Franc (1968), "Lombardy's Lakes, Blue Jewels in Italy's Crown," *National Geographic* 134 (1), July, pp. 58–99.

Shor, Jean, and Franc Shor (1954), "North with Finland's Lapps," *National Geographic* 106 (2), August, pp. 249–280.

Shor, Jean, and Franc Shor (1955), "Spain's 'Fortunate Isles,' the Canaries," *National Geographic* 107 (4), April, pp. 485–522.

Silva, Ana Paula, and Graham Hall (2005), "Influences on the Growth of Portuguese SMEs," in Alain Fayolle, Paula Kyrö, and Jan Ulijn, eds., *Entrepreneurship Research in Europe,* Cheltenham, United Kingdom: Edward Elgar, pp. 331–350.

Simões, Vitor Corado (2004), *Annual Innovation Policy for Portugal,* Brussels: European Commission, Enterprise Directorate-General.

Smiley, Xan (2001), "A Survey of Italy," insert in *The Economist,* July 7.

Sombart, Werner (1913), *The Jews and Modern Capitalism,* translated by M. Epstein, London and Leipsic: T. Fisher Unwin.

Sombart, Werner (1922), *Der moderne Kapitalismus: Historisch-systematische Darstellung des gesamteuropäischen Wirtschaftslebens von seinen Anfängen bis zur Gegenwart,* Munich and Leipsic: Duncker & Humblot.

Spencer, Jennifer W., Thomas P. Murtha, and Stefanie Ann Lenway (2005), "How Governments Matter to New Venture Creation," *Academy of Management Review* 30 (2), April, pp. 321–337.

Staley, Eugene, and Richard Morse (1971), "Developing Entrepreneurship: Elements for a Program," in Peter Kilby, ed., *Entrepreneurship and Economic Development,* New York: Free Press, pp. 374–384.

Stamp, L. Dudley (1939), *A Commercial Geography,* London: Longmans, Green and Co.

Steinmann, Horst, and Andreas Georg Scherer (2003), "Managing the Multinational Enterprise in a World of Different Cultures: Some Fundamental Remarks on the Pluralism of Cultures and Its Managerial Consequences," in Marina Ricciardelli, Sabine Urban, and Kostas Nanopoulos, eds., *Globalization and Its Multicultural Society: Some Views from Europe,* Notre Dame, Indiana: University of Notre Dame, pp. 75–101.

Sternberg, Rolf (2003), "Das Konzept endogener Regionalentwicklung — Implikationen für Existenzgründungen und deren Förderung," in Rolf Sternberg, ed., *Endogene Regionalentwicklung durch Existenzgründungen? Empirische Befunde aus Nordrhein-Westfalen,* Hannover: Akademie für Raumforschung und Landesplanung.

Sternberg, Rolf (2005), "Entrepreneurship in German Regions and the Policy Dimension," in David. B. Audretsch, Heike Grimm, and Charles W. Wessner, eds., *Local Heroes in the Global Village,* New York: Springer, pp. 113–144.

Sternberg, Rolf, Heiko Bergmann, and Christine Tamásy (2001), *Global Entrepreneurship Monitor: Länderbericht Deutschland,* Cologne: Universität zu Köln.

Sternberg, Rolf, and Ingo Lückgen (2005), *Global Entrepreneurship Monitor (GEM). Länderbericht Deutschland 2004.* Cologne: Wirtschafts-und Sozialgeographisches Institut, Universität zu Köln.

Sternberg, Rolf, Claus Otten, and Christine Tamásy (2000), *Global Entrepreneurship Monitor: Germany 2000 Country Report,* Cologne: Universität zu Köln.

Sternberg, Rolf, and Joachim Wagner (2004), "The Decision to Start a New Firm: Personal and Regional Determinants: Empirical Evidence from the Regional Entrepreneurship Monitor (REM) Germany," in Michael Fritsch, and Michael Niese, eds., *Gründungsprozess und Gründungserfolg: Interdisziplinäre Beiträge zum Entrepreneurship Research,* Heidelberg: Physica, pp. 19–38.

Strinati, Dominic (1982), *Capitalism: The State and Industrial Relations,* London: Croom Helm.

Suárez-Villa, Luis, and Ruth Rama (1996), "Outsourcing, R&D and the Pattern of Intra-Metropolitan Location: the electronics industries of Madrid," *Urban Studies* 33 (1), pp. 155–197.

Susiluoto, Klaus (2003), "The City of Oulu — A Quantum Leap into the Future," *Nordicum Scandinavian Business Magazine* 2, pp. 6–7.

Szyperski, Norbert, and Heinz Klandt (1981), "The Empirical Research on Entrepreneurship in the Federal Republic of Germany," in Karl H. Vesper, ed., *Frontiers of Entrepreneurship Research,* Wellesley, Massachusetts: Babson Center for Entrepreneurial Studies, pp. 158–178.

Turi, Johan Mathis (2002), "The World Reindeer Livelihood — Current Situation, Threats and Possibilities," in Sakari Kankaanpää, Ludger Müller-Wille, Paulo Susiluoto, and Marja-Liisa Sutinen, eds., *Northern Timberline Forests: Environmental and Socio-economic Issues and Concerns,* Kolari, Finland: The Finnish Forest Research Institute, pp. 70–75.

Ulijn, Jan, and Terrence E. Brown (2004), "Innovation, Entrepreneurship and Culture, a Matter of Interaction between Technology, Process and Economic Growth? An Introduction," in Terence E. Brown, and Jan Ulijn, eds., *Innovation, Entrepreneurship and Culture: The interaction between technology, progress and economic growth,* Cheltenham, United Kingdom: Edward Elgar, pp. 1–38.

Ulijn, Jan, and Alain Fayolle (2004), "Towards Cooperation between European Start-ups: The position of the French, German, and Dutch entrepreneurial and innovative engineer," in Terence E. Brown, and Jan Ulijn, eds., *Innovation, Entrepreneurship and Culture: The interaction between technology, progress and economic growth,* Cheltenham, United Kingdom: Edward Elgar, pp. 204–232.

Ulijn, Jan, and Hans J. M. G. Heerkens (1999), "The Death of an Innovative Firm Fokker: Were There Cultural Reasons?" *Journal of Enterprising Culture* 7 (3), pp. 269–298.

Ulijn, Jan, Arie P. Nagel, and Wee Liang Tan (2001), "The Impact of National, Corporate and Professional Cultures on Innovation: German and Dutch Firms Compared," *Journal of Enterprising Culture* 9 (1), pp. 21–52.

Van Auken, Howard E., and Domingo Garcia Perez de Lema (2003), "Financial Strategies of Spanish Firms: A Comparative Analysis by Size of Firm," *Journal of Small Business and Entrepreneurship* 17 (1), Fall, pp. 17–30.

Vidal, Jean-Philippe (1995), "PME-Hypermarchés," *Libre-Service Actualités* 16, March, pp. 28–34.

Villiers, Alan (1954), "Golden Beaches of Portugal," *National Geographic* 106 (5), November, pp. 673–696.

Villiers, Alan (1968), "The Netherlands: Nation at War With the Sea," *National Geographic* 133 (4), April, pp. 530–571.

Volery, Thierry, and Isabelle Servais (2001), *Global Entrepreneurship Monitor Rapport 2000 sur l'Entrepreneuriat en France*, Lyon: EM Lyon.

Wagner, Joachim (2004), "Are Young and Small Firms Hothouses for Nascent Entrepreneurs? Evidence from German Micro Data," *Applied Economics Quarterly* 50 (4), pp. 379–391.

Wagner, Joachim (2005), "Nascent Entrepreneurs: Institute for the Study of Labor IZA Discussion Paper 1293," in Simon C. Parker, ed., *The Life Cycle of Entrepreneurial Ventures* (International Handbook Series on Entrepreneurship, Volume 3), New York: Springer.

Wagner, Joachim, and Rolf Sternberg (2004), "Start-up Activities, Individual Characteristics, and the Regional Milieu: Lessons for Entrepreneurship Support Policies from German Micro Data," *The Annals of Regional Science* 38, pp. 219–240.

Wagner, Joachim, and Rolf Sternberg (2005), "Personal and Regional Determinants of Entrepreneurial Activities: Empirical Evidence from the Regional Entrepreneurship Monitor (REM)," *Jahrbuch für Regionalwissenschaft* 25 (1), pp. 91–105.

Walker, Harrison Howell (1940), "France Farms as War Wages: An American Explores the Rich Rural Region of the Historic Paris Basin," *National Geographic* 77 (2), February, pp. 201–238.

Walker, Howell (1958), "Belgium Welcomes the World: Millions of Visitors to the 1958 World's Fair in Brussels See an Atomic-age Exposition in a Time-mellowed Land," *National Geographic* 113 (6), June, pp. 795–838.

Walker, Howell (1963), "Italian Riviera, Land That Winter Forgot," *National Geographic* 123 (6), June, pp. 743–790.

Walker, Howell (1965), "France Meets the Sea in Brittany: Headland of Europe, the Province of the Bretons Retains its Medieval Look, its Sea-washed Air, and its Misty Light as it Harnesses the Tides and Talks with Space," *National Geographic* 127 (4), April, pp. 470–503.

Walsh, James S., and Philip H. Anderson (1995), "Owner-Manager Adaptation/Innovation Preference and Employment Performance: A Comparison of Founders and Non-Founders in the Irish Small Firm Sector," *Journal of Small Business Management* 33 (3), July, pp. 1–8.

Wanzenböck, Herta (1998), *Überleben und Wachstum junger Unternehmen*, Vienna and New York: Springer.

Weber, Max (1930), *The Protestant Ethic and the Spirit of Capitalism,* translated by Talcott Parsons, New York: Charles Scribner's Sons.

Welter, Friederike (2004), "The Environment for Female Entrepreneurship in Germany," *Journal of Small Business and Enterprise Development* 11 (2), pp. 212–221.

Welter, Friederike (2006), "Women Entrepreneurship in Germany: Progress in a Still Traditional Environment," in Candida Brush, Nancy Carter, Elizabeth B. Gatewood, Patricia C. Greene, and Myra Hart, eds., *Growth Oriented Women Entrepreneurs and Their Businesses,* Cheltenham, United Kingdom: Edward Elgar.

Welter, Friederike (2007), "Entrepreneurship in East and West Germany," *International Journal of Entrepreneurship and Small Business* 4.

Wennekers, Sander, and Roy Thurik (2001), "Institutions, Entrepreneurship and Economic Performance," in Anders Lundström and Lois Stevenson, eds., *Entrepreneurship Policy for the Future,* Stockholm: Swedish Foundation for Small Business Research, pp. 51–87.

Whitaker, Ian (1955), *Social Relations in a Nomadic Lappish Community,* Oslo: Utgitt av Norsk Folkemuseum.

White, Peter T. (1980), "Greece," *National Geographic* 157 (3), March, pp. 360–393.

Williams, Maynard Owen (1930a), "New Greece, the Centenarian, Forges Ahead," *National Geographic* 58 (6), December, pp. 649–721.

Williams, Maynard Owen (1930b), "Paris in the Spring," *National Geographic* 70 (4), October, pp. 501–534.

Williams, Maynard Owen (1946), "Paris Lives Again," *National Geographic* 150 (6), December, pp. 767–790.

Williamson, Hugh (2004), "Subtle Divisions that Mark a Reunited City," *Financial Times*, Thursday, September 23, p. 11.

Wilpert, Czarina (2003), "Germany: From Workers to Entrepreneurs," in Robert Kloosterman and Jan Rath, eds., *Immigrant Entrepreneurs: Venturing Abroad in the Age of Globalization,* Oxford: Berg, pp. 233–260.

Windebank, Jan (1991), *The Informal Economy in France,* Aldershot, United Kingdom: Avebury.

Wirtschaftskammern Österreichs (2003): *Zahlen, Daten, Fakten. Wirtschaftsgrafik 2003. Ein statistischer Rückblick* (Numbers, Data, Facts, Economic Graphic 2003: A statistical review), Vienna: Austrian Federal Economic Chamber.

Wirtschaftskammern Österreichs (2004), *Statistisches Jahrbuch 2004,* Vienna: Austrian Federal Economic Chamber.

Wirtschaftskammer Österreich (2005), "Unternehmensneugründungen in Österreich 1993 — 2004," accessed April 28, 2005 from: http://wko.at/statistik/Extranet/ Neugr/ng2004v-gesamt.pdf.

Wolf-Knuts, Ulrika (2001), "The Finland Swedes: A Compensating Minority," paper presented at Migration, Minorities, Compensation: Issues of Cultural Identity in Europe conference, Certosa di Pontigniano, March, pp. 143–152.

Zwingle, Erla (1995), "Venice: More Than a Dream," *National Geographic* 187 (2), February, pp. 73–99.

Index